THE BLACK PANTHER PARTY

SERVICE TO THE PEOPLE PROGRAMS

D1714621

The Black Panther Party

Service to the People Programs

The Dr. Huey P. Newton Foundation

Edited and with an Afterword by David Hilliard

Foreword by Cornel West

UNIVERSITY OF NEW MEXICO PRESS || ALBUQUERQUE

12　11　　　　　　　　2　3　4　5

LIBRARY OF CONGRESS CATALOGING-IN-PUBLICATION DATA

The Black Panther Party : service to the people programs /
the Dr. Huey P. Newton Foundation ; edited and with an afterword
·　by David Hilliard ; foreword by Cornel West.
p. cm.
ISBN 978-0-8263-4394-9 (pbk. : alk. paper)
1. African Americans—Services for—California—Oakland.
2. Poor—Services for—California—Oakland.
3. Community life—California—Oakland.
4. Black Panther Party—History.
5. African Americans—California—Oakland—Societies, etc.
6. African Americans—Societies, etc.
7. African Americans—Politics and government—20th century.
I. Hilliard, David. II. Dr. Huey P. Newton Foundation.
HV3185.O35B55'2008
362.8496'073079466—dc22

2007047984

Book and cover design and type composition by Kathleen Sparkes
This book was composed using Adobe Minion Pro OTF 10/14, 26P
Display type is Berthold Akzidenz Grotesk

We had seen Watts rise up the previous year. We had seen how the police attacked the Watts community after causing the trouble in the first place. We had seen Martin Luther King come to Watts in an effort to calm the people, and we had seen his philosophy of nonviolence rejected. Black people had been taught nonviolence; it was deep in us. What good, however, was nonviolence when the police were determined to rule by force? We had seen the Oakland police and the California Highway Patrol begin to carry their shotguns in full view as another way of striking fear into the community. We had seen all this, and we recognized that the rising consciousness of Black people was almost at the point of explosion. One must relate to the history of one's community and to its future. Everything we had seen convinced us that our time had come . . .

Huey P. Newton, "The Founding of the Black Panther Party," taken from his autobiography, *Revolutionary Suicide*

Contents

Foreword

The emergence of the Black Panther Party in Oakland, California, in 1966 was one of the great moments in the history of the struggle for Black freedom and deep democracy in the United States of America. This courageous and visionary group of young Black people decided to highlight the fundamental pillar of white supremacy and antidemocratic practice against Black people—namely, the vicious and unaccountable repressive actions of white police power over Black folk. Like Ida B. Wells-Barnett's heroic stance against the red terror of lynching and Jim Crow over a century ago, the Black Panther Party tried to exert democratic control over the arbitrary public violence of the U.S. nation-state that maimed and murdered Black citizens. Such organized efforts are rare in American history because they always result in Black leaders and activists paying the ultimate price of death and destruction. The Black Panther Party—led by Huey Newton, Bobby Seale, David Hilliard, and others—took up this gallant challenge in the midst of the great awakening in the 1960s.

The founding of the precious experiment of democracy in the United States was based, in large part, on the niggerization of African peoples. This centuries-long process of niggerization was not simply the enslavement and exploitation of Black people. It also aimed to keep Black people scared, intimidated, disrespectful, and distrustful of each other and doomed to helplessness and hopelessness. The basic goals of niggerization were to promote white greed and hatred; its primary strategies to secure these goals were racist ideology that degrades and devalues Black people and racist violence that terrorizes Black people. The threat to American apartheid led by Martin Luther King Jr. and Malcolm X in the '60s initiated a great democratic awakening, especially among young Black people. This awakening was the deniggerization of Black people—the process of turning scared, intimidated, helpless folk into bold, brave, hopeful people willing to live and die for Black freedom.

The Black Panther Party was the most advanced organized effort to exemplify this awakening. In other words, it was the highest form of deniggerization in niggerized America. The Black Panther Party was the greatest threat to American apartheid because it was indigenous in composition, interracial in strategies and tactics, and international in vision and analysis. It was indigenous in that it spoke to the needs and hopes of the local community, as can be seen in the historic Survival Program of the party. It combined bread-and-butter issues of everyday people with deep democratic empowerment in the face of an oppressive status quo. It was interracial in that it remained open to strategic alliances and tactical coalitions with progressive brown, red, yellow, and white activists. And it was international in that it understood American apartheid in light of anti-imperial struggles around the world, especially in Asia, Africa, and Latin America. The revolutionary politics of the Black Panther Party linked the catastrophic conditions of local Black communities (with the disgraceful school systems, unavailable health and child care, high levels of unemployment and underemployment, escalating rates of imprisonment, and pervasive forms of self-hatred and self-destruction) to economic inequality in America and colonial or neocolonial realities in the capitalist world-system. Needless to say, this great awakening was too much for the American establishment. The FBI-led war against the Black Panther Party led to Black death and destruction.

Yet forty years later, the phoenix now rises from the ashes. We will never forget the vision, courage, and sacrifice of the Black Panther Party's gallant effort to view the people's needs as holy, people's power as democratic, and people's hopes as precious. Indeed, so holy, democratic, and precious that we now struggle for a new great awakening that shatters the sleepwalking in our own time. And the Black Panther Party remains the enabling and ennobling wind at our backs!

Cornel West
Princeton University

Introduction

Emerging from the tumultuous first half of the 1960s, the founding of the Black Panther Party by Huey P. Newton and Bobby Seale in October 1966 marked the beginning of a new era for a tired, troubled, and confused America. One phrase, simultaneously both a flat statement of resistance to impoverished conditions of life and a stirring cry to action to change those conditions, best characterizes and sums up this new epoch. It was a phrase initiated by the Black Panther Party in its early days in Oakland, California, which spread like wildfire across this land—north, east, south, and west—calling forth the emergence of hitherto unknown numbers of Black, poor, and dispossessed people into conscious political activity, in their own name and in their own interests. Five simple words seized America's soul in an attempt to make it whole: "All Power to the People!"

From its founding, the Black Panther Party for Self-Defense (the phrase "for Self-Defense" was later dropped) has been assailed and vilified in the mass media, its leaders hounded and harassed by local and federal law enforcement agencies, and its membership and supporters threatened and intimidated at every turn. Through it all, the Black Panther Party has survived.

The reasons for this phenomenal resiliency in the face of tremendous obstacles and odds lies, in the final analysis, with the people—the communities served by the Black Panther Party programs and who, in turn, sustain the Black Panther Party through their heartfelt contributions of time and energy, devotion and love. In short, People's Power: that boundless and bold enthusiasm carefully and cautiously granted to those who serve the people's interest.

Contrary to misleading stories and scandalous misrepresentations, the Black Panther Party did not originate simply as an armed and violent response to police brutality and murder. The Black Panther Party is not, and never has been, a group of angry young Black "militants" full of hatred and fury toward the White Establishment.

Rather, from the outset in 1966, when Huey P. Newton and other early party members began their historic patrols of the Oakland Police Department armed with law books to explain to members of the community their basic constitutional rights, the Black Panther Party has attempted to provide an example to the community of what is possible and to raise the people's political consciousness so that we can all step forward with dignity and courage.

Programs and Achievements

Let us turn to the programs and achievements of the Black Panther Party and try to assess them for what they really are. Free Breakfast for Schoolchildren, the most well-known Black Panther Party program, is actually only one of nearly two dozen ongoing community-based activities and programs that the Black Panther Party sponsors. We have also included in this volume poetry, songs, and artwork that together make up the basis for a new, progressive People's Culture, one that roots itself in the notions of friendship and cooperation between all people. Last, in a section of book excerpts, we present the theoretical analysis that underlies the Black Panther Party and its programs.

Although this does not present the whole story, we, the editors of the fall *CoEvolution Quarterly*, feel confident knowing that task is not ours. The final chapter, yet unwritten, belongs to the people—all humankind—as they forge through their own efforts and lives a world free of the troubles that plague us today. All we can do is record their magnificent achievements.

All Power to the People

PART I
Survival Pending Revolution

Introduction to the
Black Panther Party Survival Programs

I n order to achieve its goals of organizing and serving Black and oppressed communities, the Black Panther Party has developed a wide variety of survival programs since the party's founding in October 1966. The programs, which cover such diverse areas as health care and food services, as well as a model school, the Intercommunal Youth Institute, are meant to meet the needs of the community until we can all move to change the social conditions that make it impossible for the people to afford the things they need and desire.

The survival programs provide another important service—they serve as a model for all oppressed people who wish to begin to take concrete actions to deal with their oppression.

In the succeeding pages, the survival programs are explained in detail, including information on the service provided by each program; the minimum equipment and facilities and minimum number of personnel required to run the program; how funds are raised for the maintenance of the program; how the community is organized to become involved; and how the community's consciousness is raised by each program.

Before the survival programs are presented, however, it is appropriate to present Huey P. Newton's eloquent description of the programs, taken from *To Die for the People*, Brother Huey's first book of essays:

> We recognized that in order to bring the people to the level
> of consciousness where they would seize the time, it would
> be necessary to serve their interests in survival by developing
> programs which would help them to meet their daily needs. For
> a long time we have had such programs not only for survival but

for organizational purposes. Now we not only have a breakfast program for schoolchildren, we have clothing programs, we have health clinics which provide free medical and dental services, we have programs for prisoners and their families, and we are opening clothing and shoe factories to provide for more of the needs of the community. Most recently we have begun a testing and research program on sickle-cell anemia; and we know that 98 percent of the victims of this disease are Black. To fail to combat this disease is to submit to genocide; to battle it is survival.

All these programs satisfy the deep needs of the community but they are not solutions to our problems. That is why we call them survival programs, meaning survival pending revolution. We say that the survival program of the Black Panther Party is like the survival kit of a sailor stranded on a raft. It helps him to sustain himself until he can get completely out of that situation. So the survival programs are not answers or solutions, but they will help us to organize the community around a true analysis and understanding of their situation. When consciousness and understanding is raised to a high level then the community will seize the time and deliver themselves from the boot of their oppressors.

All of our survival programs are free. We have never charged the community a dime to receive the things they need from any of our programs and we will not do so. We will not get caught up in a lot of embarrassing questions or paperwork which alienate the people. If they have a need we will serve their needs and attempt to get them to understand the true reasons why they are in need in such an incredibly rich land. Survival programs will always be operated without charge to those who need them and benefit by them . . .

Intercommunal Youth Institute

The Intercommunal Youth Institute was established in January 1971 by the Black Panther Party. The institute was initiated in direct response to the public school system, which has systematically produced individuals totally incapable of thinking in an analytical way. The failure of the public school system to educate Black and poor youth has caused generation after generation of our people to be inadequately prepared to participate and survive in our highly technological society. In order to begin to break this seemingly endless cycle of oppression, the Black Panther Party established the Youth Institute. Our plan is to provide an example in the education of Black children and to guide our children toward becoming fully capable of analyzing the problems they will face and to develop creative solutions to deal with them.

Since 1971, the institute has almost doubled in its enrollment and has developed its program more fully. Today the institute includes more than one hundred youth from the ages of two and a half to eleven. They are children of Black Panther Party members as well as children of people from throughout the greater Oakland community. Our concentration is not only on providing basic skills and an analytical way of thinking; we also seek to transform the way in which the youth interrelate with each other. The young people at the school are regarded as developing human beings whose ideas and opinions are respected. Via the Youth Committee, the youth participate in a democratic fashion in planning many school activities. They may openly criticize the entire program of our school, using as their guide the basic principles of living and working together in harmony.

Each One Teach One

The instructors and students have mutual love and respect for one another; both understand the need for the principle "each one help one; each one teach

The Black Panther Youth, Oakland, California, 1972. Photo by Stephen Shames.

one." They live, work, and play together. Everything is done collectively in order to develop an understanding of solidarity and camaraderie in a practical way. Since education is an ongoing twenty-four-hour process, all of the parents of the youth work very closely with the institute. Parents are encouraged to give suggestions and make criticisms at the institute's weekly meetings, both of which are essential to our progress.

The academic program of the institute covers a wide variety of subject matter. The following courses are taught:

Math—The math classes are intended to develop the concept of a set, to introduce the number line, and to enable children to understand that measurements are a form of comparison for matching the object or quantity being measured. Mathematical formulas and concepts are being taught and tested in various experiments such as cooking and a school store, which the children have begun.

We, who already belong, in most senses, to past generations are obliged, it seems, to transfer our heritage of knowledge to succeeding generations for their survival. This is generally called education. However, it is not, I believe, our duty to impose our limited interpretation of this past on the next generation. Surely the future belongs to those who will live it.

It is in this spirit [that] the Intercommunal Youth Institute seeks to educate Black and poor youth. The Intercommunal Youth Institute's primary task, then, is not so much to transmit a received doctrine from past experience as [it is] to provide the young with the ability and technical training that will make it possible for them to evaluate their heritage for themselves; to translate what is known into their own experiences and thus discover more readily their own.

Black and poor youth in this country have been offered a blurred vision of the future through unenlightened and racist educational institutions. The institute is the realization of a dream, then, to repair disabled minds and the disenfranchised lives of this country's poor communities, to lay the foundations as to create an arena for the world without such suffering. Our aim is to provide the young of these communities with as much knowledge [as] possible and to provide them with the ability to interpret that knowledge with understanding. For we believe without knowledge there can be no real understanding and that understanding is the key to liberation of all.

Huey P. Newton

Language Arts—The purpose of this class is to enable children to learn at an early age sounds, symbols, consonants, vowels, and reading comprehension. The children are taught to utilize their knowledge in reading such relevant material as newspapers, brochures, leaflets, as well as textbooks. Our major concern is that the children read, comprehend, and retain.

MATTER AND ENERGY

Science—The focus of the science classes is to inform the children of the concepts of matter, energy, and biology. Awareness of self is a crucial preliminary stage to the understanding of scientific principles and is a major area of learning within the science courses. The children learn to know the balance between man and nature as well as other scientific knowledge necessary to exist in a highly technological and scientific world.

People's Art—The purpose of this class is to bring out the creative abilities of each student through artistic expression. The history of art and painting, its relationship to Black and poor people, and field trips are the focus of this course.

Political Education—The purpose of this class is to teach the children how and why it is necessary to be critical of the situation the world is in, to foster an investigative attitude, and to provide a framework for the comparison of different peoples and their politics. American history as well as Black and Mexican American history are included here.

WORLD A CLASSROOM

Environmental Studies—One of the basic philosophies of the Intercommunal Youth Institute holds that the community and the world are classrooms wherein learning occurs through observation and experience as well as study. Many field trips have taken place during the past three months, including trips to the Zen Center, Green Gulch Farm at Tassajara, the San Francisco Legion of Honor Museum, the de Young Museum in San Francisco, and to the Bay Area Hydraulic Model. More field trips are planned for the future so that the children can benefit from a total learning experience.

A wide variety of methods are utilized in teaching the various subjects. Two basic principles underline and run through all of the classes. First, the general analytical approach in all subject areas is one of understanding the many-sidedness of all things as opposed to a one-sided or narrow view of reality. Therefore, the youth view things in a practical, nonidealistic manner. Their understanding of the world will lead them to investigation and analysis of both the positive and negative aspects of a thing.

The second principle that is emphasized is that in order to be able to transform any situation or thing, one must be in contact with it. The youth at various times study the physical and social phenomena of their community firsthand and test out their theories for making basic changes through practical activity.

The staff of the Intercommunal Youth Institute consists of nineteen men and women who perform the task of teaching the youth. Since classes at the institute are arranged in groups, (Groups I to VII) with the children passing from one grade to another according to their ability rather than according to their age, the staff are not locked into a fixed pattern.

Take the instructors for Groups I, II, and III, for example. For these three groups, the basic curriculum consists of language arts, mathematics, reading, writing, and sensory motor skills. With a program like this, the instructors cannot adhere to rigid or "traditional" teaching techniques.

The staff at the institute consists of both accredited and nonaccredited teachers; although credentials certainly do not always interrelate with ability, the nonaccredited staff takes college courses to gain degrees and attain more teaching skills.

In addition to the day-to-day staff, several consultants who are all well-respected in the field of childhood education donate their time to advance the smooth flow of work and understanding at the Intercommunal Youth Institute. In September 1974, Bill Moore, a former professor at the University of Santa Cruz, began coordinating the curriculum development at the school. Also working in the role of consultants are Chuck Lawrence, former principal of an alternative school in Boston and presently an attorney with the prestigious Public Advocates Office in San Francisco, and Herb Kohl, author of *Open Classroom* and *36 Children* and the director of the Center for Open Learning in Berkeley. Several of the teachers from the institute have attended training sessions, workshops, and classes under Mr. Kohl's direction.

The initial funding for the institute's first year at the Community Learning Center was provided by the Economic Opportunities Corporation, a nonprofit group, and through the contributions from the Daniel J. Berstein Foundation, Pacific Change, the Youth Project, the Third World Fund, and the Genesis Church and Ecumenical Center. Many private contributors including Tom and Flora Gladwin, Bert Schneider, Stanley K. Sheinbaun, and Candice Bergen have also given financial assistance.

The institute has also launched a campaign to gain financial support for the students at the school through pledges to the Each One Teach One Tuition Association. Monies donated on a monthly, quarterly, biannually, or yearly basis are used to directly support the youth.

In addition to financial assistance, the Intercommunal Youth Institute is seeking much-needed supplies such as playground equipment, new books, toys, clothes, and general school supplies. People and businesses with access to school materials are asked to help by donating any of these supplies to the school. All donations are tax-deductible.

Community Learning Center

The Community Learning Center (CLC) is a multipurpose people's institution providing progressive educational, cultural, and social activities. Sponsored by the Educational Opportunities Corporation, a nonprofit (tax-exempt) association of civic-minded Bay Area residents, the Community Learning Center is located in the heart of the East Oakland Black community.

Besides housing both the Intercommunal Youth Institute and the Son of Man Temple, the CLC sponsors a number of after-school and evening programs that touch the lives of hundreds of East Oakland residents. These programs include a Cultural Arts Program, which provides skilled instruction in music, dance, and drama; a women's self-defense class; and an Adult Education Program. In addition, the CLC has been privileged to host a broad variety of community events, ranging from rallies to topflight professional entertainment, as well as provide a meeting place for local grassroots political groups.

But, above all, the CLC is a community center for the youth—children of all ages—whose development as conscious and aware human beings fills the CLC staff with pride.

Cultural Arts Program

Music—Creativity, commitment, and motivation have been the key elements responsible for the rapid progress of the Music Program. Since its inception, three performing units (the combo, trio, and Intercommunal Youth Band), comprised of children who had never before handled a musical instrument, have been formed. Performances are held each Sunday at the Son of Man Temple as well as at schools and various community affairs in the Bay Area.

The Black Panther Party Liberation School, Oakland, California, 1972. Names and photographer unknown.

Students at the Intercommunal Youth Institute are active participants in the Music Program and children from the public schools come to the after-school program with their own instruments for instruction. According to Charles Moffett, the well-known director of the program, who is the former music director for the city of Oakland and who once performed with the late John Coltrane, these children hold "first chair" positions in their public school orchestras. This indicates that their instruction at the Community Learning Center is very beneficial.

This past spring, in fact, the Intercommunal Youth Band won the first-prize award in the FESTAC '74 contest, earning themselves the opportunity to perform in the national contest in New York City this fall and opening up the possibility of a trip to Lagos, Nigeria, for the international FESTAC '75 contest.

Dance—The Dance Program, directed by Jackie Buist, is divided into two sections. Children from ages five to seven are taught the basics of African dance. African rhythms are taught with the use of tambourines, bells, and drums.

Children from ages eight to thirteen are taught Afro-Haitian dance, utilizing the Kathryn Dunheim technique. African, Cuban, and Brazilian dances are taught and the youth will be expected to make up their own dances once the basics are learned.

Drama—Expression of Black people's culture and lifestyles through drama is the essence of the drama classes, which Eugene Frazier instructs at the Community Learning Center. Drama, which is concerned with realism in the community, can foster community awareness and a heightened level of consciousness. This program is open to everyone over twelve years old.

Children in this program are being taught basic theory, including background in the creative arts' historical developments of Black people's culture, speech development, stage management, and reading. This theory will then be utilized and combined with actual live performances.

This course will afford children an outlet for free expression and will present entertainment with an educational content to the community.

Women's Self-Defense Class—Tae Kwon Do, a form of karate, is being taught at the Learning Center by Brother Luther Sucrease. Brother Sucrease holds a black belt in karate and is a member of the Wado-Kai Association, which is a national body of practitioners of Wado-Kai.

This class concerns itself with two aspects of self-defense. One is mental: being able to understand the philosophy of determination, self-respect, and discipline. The physical aspect involves numerous stretching exercises and instruction on proper breathing control and endurance.

Adult Education Program—Every Tuesday and Thursday from 7 to 9 p.m., Maureen Knightly conducts classes for adults who wish to acquire a high school General Equivalency Diploma (GED). The Community Learning Center, in affiliation with the Oakland Board of Education, is offering courses to help people prepare for the necessary exam for this diploma. Courses include basic reading, writing, and math.

It is anticipated that the Adult Education Program will be extended to include consumer education, home economics, courses for senior citizens, and other courses that Black and poor residents desperately need.

Physically, the Community Learning Center is a large structure (a transformed Baptist church), with an auditorium that seats three hundred, kitchen facilities for 250, and twenty-five classrooms and meeting rooms. A large parking lot in the rear of the facility can hold more than one hundred cars.

The CLC is financed by community support, special fund-raising activities, individual contributions, and private foundation grants.

As examples of the types of fund-raising activities planned, both Oscar Brown Jr. and Ms. Aminata Moseka (Abbey Lincoln) have performed at CLC benefits, providing the community with outstanding, quality entertainment and drawing much-needed funds for the CLC programs. Rentals for the CLC auditorium have produced such memorable rallies as the International Women's Day event this past spring and a "justice for Tyrone Guyton" rally (a fourteen-year-old Black youth killed by Emeryville police) in February. In conjunction with the CLC, Laney College sponsored a weekly Black film series in the auditorium.

Cost

Of course, more financial support is always needed because the operational cost of the Intercommunal Youth Institute alone is approximately six thousand dollars per month, totaling seventy-two thousand dollars per year. The approximate operating cost of the entire Community Learning Center is one hundred thousand dollars per year.

Community personnel are incorporated throughout the CLC in the planning and implementation of its programs as office personnel and as enthusiastic participants in the CLC programs.

Son of Man Temple

Statement of Purpose

We have always hoped that we could establish a place in our community where hundreds of ideas could grow and flourish, where people could feel free to say and do the things that seemed most natural to them. The Son of Man Temple was created for that purpose, to serve in humankind's development.

However, the place in which we come together to express our humanity is not a church in the most traditional sense. We do not practice a religion; we are not Christian, Jewish, Buddhist, Hindu, or Moslem. We do not honor one God or one reverend. This does not mean that we negate any religion; we all have differing philosophies and views of our world. We are all a part of everything and it is a part of each of us.

Our belief is that every human being has the right to be free. We can all agree that we are not. Therefore, we come together to express our agreement on that belief every Sunday at the Son of Man Temple. It is a place where we can come to discover and learn. If we begin the week with this kind of unity and understanding, we can carry through each day our concern and an enthusiastic feeling about our survival and our freedom.

The ways in which we express this agreement about our desire to break away from our common problem—oppression—may differ. Some of us might sing or dance about it, some of us might play music about it, or some of us might speak about various aspects of our problem. It does not matter what we do if it is done with sincerity and in our people's interest. Our intent is not to simply talk or sing. We will, through various community programs in action at the Learning Center, which houses our temple, create the means of solving the problems we face.

The Son of Man Temple must become known as a community forum, a place where the dreams of the people can become ideas, where ideas can become a practical reality, where that reality will lead us forward to freedom.

Our purpose, then, is to come together, let our differences be minimized, and let our similarities blossom. We want the belief that we should live, that our children should live, that our people should live, to be contagious. We want our belief in the beauty of life to spread to freedom-loving people everywhere.

Let us use this place, this temple, to be happy together, not about our oppression, but happy because we recognize that we are oppressed and have gotten together to throw off that oppression.

The Son of Man Temple is dedicated to community survival in particular and to the development of humankind in general. It is:

1) A community forum held every Sunday with a format covering historical and contemporary subject matters as they relate to the needs and desires of the community. The uniqueness of the forum includes invited guest speakers who deliver the key address/message. These speakers come from areas such as poverty agencies, community colleges and universities, civic organizations, media, local associations, and community residents who would like to share their knowledge and experiences. The program, called "celebration services," for that in essence is what they are, is highlighted with the presentation of a guest artist (local and professional) who provides topflight entertainment ranging from instrumental and vocal music to poetry, recitals, dance, and drama troupes.

2) A vehicle to provide and help create concrete programs in the interest of community survival. Some of the programs that the Son of Man Temple helped create or provide facilities for are:

   A. Auditorium or gathering hall with minimum of 100–150 seating capacity

   B. Ability to accommodate a wide range of various forms of entertainment (i.e., bands, dance groups, vocalists, fashion troupes)

   C. Staff of competent personnel to do clerical, technical, and administrative chores (i.e., usher board, hostess committee, speakers and entertainment committee, information committee, public address technicians)

Funding

Funding to sustain the meeting hall and programs of the temple is primarily obtained from collections at the regular weekly services held each Sunday.

Through tithes of a given sum committed by return members of the congregation, the collections each week can be allocated for general use or specific programs and projects.

The hostess committee is another prime source of fund-raising. The task of organizing bake sales, car washes, and other labor-donated services, utilizing all types of resources, is the responsibility of this group.

Due to the nonprofit nature of the temple, the soliciting of sponsorship through local community businesses and other financial sources is another means of raising revenue. The donor who can recover the contribution as a tax write-off also benefits.

Dedication and Celebration

A packed audience enjoyed the grand dedication celebration of the new location of the Son of Man Temple and Intercommunal Youth Institute at 6118 East 14th Street, in the heart of East Oakland, California, on October 21, 1973. An array of talented children, entertainers, and noted community leaders participated in the ceremonies, described by one excited mother as "a look into the future."

Seniors Against a Fearful Environment (SAFE)

Seniors Against a Fearful Environment (SAFE), a nonprofit corporation, was begun by the Black Panther Party at the request of a group of senior citizens for the purpose of preventing muggings and attacks upon the elderly, particularly when they go out to cash their meager social security or pension checks. Prior to approaching the Black Panther Party, the seniors had gone to the Oakland Police Department to request protection. There the seniors were told, to their dismay and outrage, that they "should walk close to the curb" in the future. Mrs. Van Frank, founder of the East Bay Legislative Council of Senior Citizens and the state of California's Outstanding Senior Citizen for 1971, commenting on the dangers experienced by the senior citizens, has remarked: "The fear engendered among us old people by these muggings almost makes us prisoners in our own homes."

A section of a recent funding proposal for the SAFE Program substantiates these claims. A comparative crime study was done over a period of six weeks (August 21 to October 1, 1972) and details conclusively that the age of the victim does bear a definite relationship to the type of offense committed. Of the combined total of 249 victims of strong-arm robbery and purse-snatching, 48 percent of the victims (118) were over the age of fifty. During this same period, only 13 percent of complainants in armed robbery cases fell into the senior citizen category. The conclusion, then, is that an elderly person is more likely to be physically attacked, whereas the younger, more agile person, who is more able to a defend his- or herself, will more likely be the victim of an armed assault. The fact has also been established that 33 percent of all crimes committed in the city of Oakland are committed against senior citizens.

Funding for the SAFE Program is particularly crucial to the program's ability to serve the needs of the elderly. Presently the program functions at the

Party volunteers regularly checked on and escorted elders to appointments. Photo ca. 1972. Location, names, and photographer unknown.

beginning of each month, offering free transportation and escort services to the residents of the Satellite Senior Homes, a residential complex exclusively for the elderly, located at 540 21st Street in Oakland. This is far from the goal. As the SAFE funding proposal outlines, the program's development will be quite extensive:

1. Provide round-the-clock transportation services (to senior citizens) in Alameda County, at no cost to low-income elderly residents who otherwise would have no means of transport . . . to do vital shopping, to keep medical appointments and other necessary commitments . . .
2. Provide delivery services of life-sustaining food, medical prescriptions, and medicines . . .

3. Provide assistance in moving household furnishings within Alameda County at no cost to low-income persons . . .
4. Provide an escort for senior citizens as they walk to and from recreational, entertainment, and social facilities and activities, in order to prevent assaults against and robberies of elderly persons . . .
5. Encourage a spirit of respect for and concern about the special needs of the elderly through the presentation of educational programs and the distribution of educational and scientific materials . . .

The SAFE Program also aims to unite Black and poor communities by actively recruiting and hiring a number of our youth to help implement these much-needed services. Both drivers and escorts will be recruited from among the young and unemployed in our community, a strategy that at the same time will cut down the number of youth who would consider snatching a pocketbook just to get a little change. In addition, drivers and escorts will be given extensive training in their respective fields, with both groups receiving intensive safety and first-aid instruction.

State, federal, and local funding of the SAFE Program will also mean additional transportation—at least five vans with a seating capacity of twelve persons each, plus the hiring of a full-time program director and assistants. All totaled, the proposed annual budget for the SAFE Program comes to slightly less than two hundred thousand dollars ($195,530).

Efforts to acquire funds for the SAFE Program have not yet been successful. A formal proposal has been presented before Oakland Model Cities, a federally funded poverty program, but that agency has made no commitment. A portion of Oakland's $4.5 million in revenue-sharing funds has been suggested for the SAFE Program, but the city administrators have been typically mum. Complete and adequate funding for the SAFE Program was, in fact, an integral part of the Seale-Brown Fourteen-Point Program to Rebuild Oakland in the 1973 campaign and, far from being abandoned, it will be included in initiatives and referendums.

The SAFE funding proposal, like the program itself, is an argument for our protection instead of our abuse by public service agencies, which theoretically function on our behalf. SAFE is a simple but basic program designed to help and secure the lives of a very important yet often forgotten segment of our communities: the older people. It was established and structured to do many creative and worthwhile things that would benefit our elderly. The city of Oakland spends over 41 percent of the city budget, close to $32 million, on public safety. Fifty-five thousand dollars were spent wastefully on a new police helicopter, yet as one senior citizen has put it, "They have a new helicopter flying around in the sky while we are being mugged on the ground."

SAFE does not only provide invaluable social services; it can also aid practically in uniting our communities. The sacrifices and blood-struggles of our old folk have sustained us in a thousand different ways. A fully developed SAFE Program, by providing necessary comforts and peace of mind when our elderly have reached the twilight of their years, will tell them that their fight was not in vain.

People's Free Medical Research Health Clinics

We believe that the government must provide, free of charge,
for the people, health facilities that will not only treat our illnesses,
most of which are a result of our oppression, but that will also develop
preventative medical programs to guarantee our future survival.
We believe that mass health education and research programs
must be developed to give all Black and oppressed people access to
advanced scientific and medical information, so we may provide
ourselves with proper medical attention and care.

Point Six of the Black Panther Party Program's Platform of March 29, 1972, explains the reasons for the institution of the People's Free Medical Research Health Clinics, which provide free medical treatment and preventative medical care for the community. Private hospitals and doctors charge fees far more expensive than poor people can afford, while public hospitals and clinics are so overcrowded and understaffed that their services are almost totally inadequate. The People's Free Medical Research Health Clinics offer an alternative to this problem.

The clinics provide comprehensive health care for the community. Doctors treat patients for common physical ailments and refer them to specialists if necessary. Laboratory testing is also provided in conjunction with local hospitals.

Along with the Sickle-Cell Anemia Research Foundation, the clinics conduct testing and research for a cure for sickle-cell anemia.

Child health is a serious problem in the Black community, and the clinics have developed a Child Health Care Program to meet this community need. The Child Health Care Program provides immunization; screening for sickle-cell anemia, iron deficiency anemia, and tuberculosis; referrals; and complete physical examinations as well as treatment of illnesses. Follow-up is key to this program, and participants are encouraged to come in for periodic checkups, and special problems are given careful ongoing attention.

A large building is needed to house an individual clinic. It may be one or two stories and will be divided into a reception area and waiting room, several diagnostic rooms, a laboratory, and one or more rooms for storage of medical supplies and other equipment.

A large medical supply is kept on hand at all times. Modern, clean medical equipment is also available to meet the variety of health requests made. A van is also needed to transport supplies, equipment, staff, and patients when necessary.

A minimum volunteer staff of ten is required to run a clinic. Three or more doctors come in at scheduled times during the week to see patients. Three attendants assist the doctors in screening and treating the patients. It is preferable that these attendants be medical students who have a high degree of skill and interest in their work. Two laboratory technicians, who should also be medical students, do all laboratory analysis necessary. One receptionist registers patients, handles telephone queries about the clinic's services, and maintains a file of individual patient records. A driver is on hand to pick up or transport medical supplies and equipment.

The People's Free Medical Research Health Clinics depend heavily on community donations for maintenance of the health services. Volunteers solicit funds from individual businessmen, churches, and social clubs, as well as conduct door-to-door campaigns to seek funds.

One technique employed for fund-raising is to set up a Community Outreach Program whereby mobile units go out into the community and conduct sickle-cell anemia testing, give polio vaccinations, and so forth. Such programs accomplish a great deal in the way of demonstrating to the community how the clinic is directly meeting the people's health needs and will hopefully encourage them to make financial contributions.

Clinic staff must maintain face-to-face contact with key staff personnel at local hospitals. Doctors are persuaded to donate their services free of charge because they see that the clinic is satisfying a need that hospitals fail to meet. Registered nurses and other medical employees may be asked to help organize the clinic's medical supplies or set up a Child Health Care Program. The utilization of their services gets them involved.

Community Encouraged

The community at large is encouraged to help set up outreach programs and establish contacts with key community leaders who may be helpful in allocating funds or equipment for the clinic.

The People's Free Medical Research Health Clinics may be a lifesaver for people who cannot afford the good quality health care that they deserve.

Through the operation of the program the community begins to see that it is possible to receive professional, competent, and, above all, preventative medical help without paying any money for it. The people also come to understand that as taxpayers they do not have to stand for the lackadaisical treatment given them by county hospitals and other public health facilities. Therefore, they begin to ask questions and to organize themselves to change existing health services so that they truly serve the people.

Sickle-Cell Anemia Research Foundation

stablished by the Black Panther Party in 1971 to test and create a cure for sickle-cell anemia (a deadly blood disease that affects primarily Black Americans), the Sickle-Cell Anemia Research Foundation informs people about sickle-cell anemia and maintains a national advisory committee of doctors to research this crippling disease.

In conjunction with the People's Free Medical Research Health Clinics, the Sickle-Cell Anemia Research Foundation to date has tested nearly half a million people throughout the country in the last three years.

While more research is needed to discover treatment and a cure for the disease, people must first be informed about it and tested to see if they have it or its side effects. To accomplish this, the Sickle-Cell Anemia Research Foundation publishes and disseminates brochures and other printed materials with facts about sickle-cell anemia.

The foundation operates a national headquarters in Oakland, California, and local offices in major cities throughout the country. Local offices require one or more mimeographing machines to handle the massive amount of printing that must be done to educate the community about sickle-cell anemia and the services offered by the foundation.

Office equipment required includes an extensive file system for records of those people tested in the outreach programs and telephones with one or more lines. In addition, one or more mobile units for the community outreach programs are needed. These units are equipped with the necessary modern equipment to conduct sickle-cell anemia testing.

The Black Panther Party sponsored free sickle-cell anemia testing. San Pablo Park, Oakland, California, March 31, 1972. Names unknown. Photo by Hank Lebo.

Volunteers

Eight volunteer personnel are necessary for the program's operation. Four people conduct the testing in the outreach program. They are either medical students or have received training in sickle-cell anemia testing from accredited hospitals. The sickle-cell testers are responsible for efficiently and accurately testing the community and recording the health background information for each person tested. They must also be sufficiently knowledgeable about the disease to answer questions intelligently, and they should pass out brochures and materials whenever possible.

Two doctors who consult with local foundations and conduct sickle-cell research are also required. The role of the doctors is to help the staff set up a workable community outreach program that will provide the most productive results. The doctors also provide the foundation with liaison hospitals that conduct sickle-cell research and that may be willing to donate some of their facilities and equipment free of charge to the foundation.

Two office personnel are responsible for handling the foundation's communications operations. Office staff must be able to answer questions about sickle-cell anemia, including basic questions relating to the disease. They must also organize and systematize the records of all persons tested in the outreach programs. They will also need to be in constant contact with hospitals that prepare the test results in order to follow up with any individuals who may be found to have the disease or its side effects.

Medical research and testing are expensive. While the Sickle-Cell Anemia Research Foundation depends on the same basic fund-raising techniques employed by the People's Free Medical Research Health Clinics, its personnel also write proposals to private foundations in order to obtain funds for the foundation's operations. By seeking funds from private organizations, the foundation may secure several thousand dollars at a time.

Involvement of community personnel is similar to that of the People's Free Medical Research Health Clinics. Clinic staff must maintain face-to-face contact with key personnel at local hospitals. Doctors are persuaded to donate their services free of charge because they see that the clinics are satisfying a need that hospitals fail to meet. Registered nurses and other medical employees may be asked to help organize the clinic's medical supplies or set up a Child Health Care Program. The utilization of their services gets them involved.

The community at large is encouraged to help set up outreach programs and establish contacts with key community leaders who may be helpful in allocating funds or equipment for the clinics.

Of the many advancements within the field of modern medicine that have taken place within the last fifty years, there has been one area of research and inquiry that has been severely neglected: sickle-cell anemia. While the government has spent large amounts of funds and a great deal of time researching such fatal diseases as leukemia and cancer, it has shown little interest in sickle-cell anemia until the last two or three years. The Black community recognizes that little research in sickle-cell anemia has been done because the disease primarily affects Black people.

The Sickle-Cell Anemia Research Foundation has raised the consciousness of the community, first by giving it the basic facts about the disease, and second by bringing to its attention the neglect of the disease in medical research. The community has learned through the foundation's program that only the people themselves can organize and find solutions to the problems that daily affect their survival.

People's Free Ambulance Service

The Black Panther Party's People's Free Ambulance Service provides free, rapid transportation for sick or injured people without time-consuming checks into the patients' financial status or means.

Adequate ambulance service has long been a problem in Black communities across this country. Hospitals either blanketly refuse to send their ambulances into Black communities or charge exorbitant prices if they do offer the service.

The People's Free Ambulance Service operates with at least one ambulance on a twenty-four-hour emergency basis, and from 8 a.m. to 5 p.m. on a nonemergency or convalescent basis. The services provided by this survival program are totally free. People are transported to and from the hospital or doctor's office in a modern, comfortable ambulance by courteous, efficient, and knowledgeable attendants.

The number of ambulances and other necessary equipment will vary with the size of the city to be serviced, but at least three to four ambulances should be used in large metropolitan areas with sizable Black communities.

Ambulances should contain oxygen equipment for those patients who may need it en route to the hospital; other health supplies such as first-aid kits; and most important, dispatch radio equipment so that the ambulance drivers can be in constant communication with headquarters. The radio equipment should be of the highest possible quality so that it will have minimal mechanical failures.

One or more nonemergency vehicles are used to transport the convalescent to the doctor, clinic, or hospital.

The ambulance program operates from a central office or headquarters. In a large metropolitan area it is best to have an office located in each major area of the city. Telephones with two or more lines will be needed for all such offices.

The People's Free Ambulance Service is operated with a strictly volunteer staff whose number will vary from city to city. However, at least two ambulance drivers and attendants should be available in addition to two persons to handle communications at the central office.

Office staff must man the telephone twenty-four hours a day. Efficient, pleasant-sounding personnel must be able to handle emergency situations and get information from people who may be emotionally upset because of the sudden illness of a loved one. It is especially important that the communications staff get exact information such as name, address, telephone number, preference of hospital, and the nature of the illness. The latter is vital because it may save the patient's life.

Once such information is obtained, the communications staff must quickly transmit it to their roving ambulances. Again, the staff must pass on information accurately because the drivers are dependent on them. Drivers should be highly skilled and have chauffeur's licenses if at all possible. They must be able to drive quickly but safely in life-or-death situations.

Ambulance attendants in the People's Free Ambulance Service complete extensive emergency medical technician (EMT) training at colleges and technical institutes in their local areas with the goal of becoming certified ambulance attendants.

Several thousand dollars are needed to purchase and maintain the ambulances, nonemergency vehicles, and other supplies needed for the People's Free Ambulance Service. In one city where the program operates (Winston-Salem, North Carolina), a grant was received from the National Episcopal Church's General Convention Special Program.

Because this program serves the health needs of the community, doctors are contacted for financial contributions or advice on where to seek funds. Hospitals may be willing to donate some equipment and can be helpful in determining the cost and in setting up the program.

The massive funds needed for the maintenance of the program make it vital for procurement personnel to visit large businesses, health, and church organizations to secure money and/or equipment. As is done in other survival programs of the Black Panther Party, fund-raising events such as concerts by popular entertainers can be organized.

For those people whose loved ones have died or languished at home because of inadequate or expensive ambulance service, the People's Free Ambulance Service meets one of the community's real needs. By benefiting from such a needed service that is free of charge, the community begins to question why hospitals charge them such high fees. Community consciousness is raised about inadequate health care in general, and the people, under the leadership of the staff of the People's Free Ambulance Service, begin to organize to correct these inadequacies.

Free Breakfast for Schoolchildren Program

I.

The Free Breakfast for Schoolchildren Program was the first survival program to be implemented by the Black Panther Party. Initiated in Oakland, California, the breakfast program provided a free, hot, and nutritionally balanced breakfast for any child who attended the program. By 1969, there were hundreds of breakfast programs throughout the country. A top government official was forced to admit, "The Panthers are feeding more kids than we are."

As was the purpose of the program, many groups, individuals, and organizations have taken the example and initiated programs of their own. Many Panther breakfast programs have been completely taken over by such groups and are functioning on their own. Guidelines for setting up a program in your home or community follow:

Sample Menu for One Week

MONDAY	WEDNESDAY	FRIDAY
Scrambled eggs	Eggs	Eggs
Grits	Home fries	Grits
Bacon	Ham	Bacon
Toast and jelly	Toast and jam	Toast and jam
Juice or milk	Milk or juice	Milk or juice

TUESDAY	THURSDAY
Hot cakes	French toast
Sausage	Bacon
Fresh fruit	Fresh fruit
Hot chocolate	Hot chocolate

Charles Bursey, Black Panther Party member, serves food for the Free Breakfast for Schoolchildren Program, Oakland, California, ca. 1970. This program inspired and laid the groundwork for the school breakfast programs that exist today. Other name unknown. Photo by Ruth-Marion Baruch.

II.

The minimum requirements for facilities and equipment include a building capable of holding at least fifty people such as a recreation center, church, or office building, and each facility must be equipped with kitchen equipment. Kitchen equipment includes a stove with at least four burners and an oven, and an adequate amount of large restaurant-size pots, pans, and serving utensils. For the purpose of serving a large number of children on a rotating basis with speed and efficiency, there must be an adequate amount of paper and plastic eating utensils such as paper cups, plates, and napkins; plastic knives, forks, and spoons. A minimum of 1,600 of each unit should be on hand to start a free breakfast program in any large poverty-stricken area.

The facility must be equipped with tables and chairs to seat fifty children at one time, and also there must be some room for seating children who may have to wait for a short while before eating.

There should be ample space to hang or place the children's cloaks, coat hangers, and so forth.

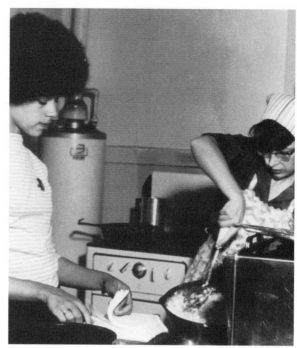

Party volunteers prepare food for the Free Breakfast for Schoolchildren Program, Oakland, California, ca. 1970. Names unknown. Photo by Ruth-Marion Baruch.

There must be ample waste disposal units on the premises. Usually two or three thirty-gallon garbage pails will be sufficient for each day's operation. Ample refrigeration and/or freezer space must be available for storing perishable foods.

There must also be a reception table set up with a sign-in book in which accurate records may be kept of names, addresses, and ages of the children who participate in the program.

III.

There should be a minimum of ten persons working on a breakfast program. Their duties should be defined as follows:

    2 persons on traffic control helping the children across the streets
    1 person doing the sign-in book operation (i.e., receptionist)
    1 person taking wraps (coats, hats)
    4 servers and table attendants
    2 cooks

Participant in the
Black Panther Party's
Free Breakfast for
Schoolchildren
Program, Oakland,
California, ca. 1970.
Name unknown.
Photo by Pirkle Jones.

IV.

Funds for operating a free breakfast program can come from a variety of sources, such as local merchants in a surrounding community, private donors, foundations, churches, and other venues.

Having the program operate out of a church has the advantage of the tax-free status of a nonprofit organization. With the church receiving the donations on behalf of the free breakfast program, letters soliciting funds and goods may be mailed out. People working with the program may openly solicit donations from businesses in the community, giving those who donate a receipt so they can legally claim their donation as a tax exemption.

V.

The best way to involve community members in the program is to let them know about the program and what its needs are. This may be done by contacting the parents of the children who come to the breakfast program. These parents may be asked to volunteer one day per week to work in the program or perhaps go out and help solicit funds or food for the program. There should also be community meetings held to explain the program and to recruit volunteers.

VI.

The program will raise consciousness in the form of people participating in a program that they put together themselves to serve themselves and their children.

People will come to understand a concept of getting businesspeople in the community to give something back to the community and do so in a way that the businesspeople can understand.

The consciousness of the children will be raised in that they will see someone outside the structure of their own family working in their interest and motivated by love and concern.

Free Food Program

The Black Panther Party's Free Food Program provides free food to Black and other oppressed people. The current spiraling of food prices makes it increasingly difficult for Black and other poor people to buy good quality, nutritious food for their families. The long-range effect of high food prices can be devastating for children who need nourishing food in order to develop strong, mentally alert adult bodies.

Huey P. Newton, leader and chief theoretician of the Black Panther Party, says in explaining the party's survival programs:

> We recognized that in order to bring the people to the level
> of consciousness where they would seize the time, it would
> be necessary to serve their interests in survival by developing
> programs that would help them to meet their daily needs . . . All
> these programs satisfy the deep needs of the community but
> they are not solutions to our problems. That is why we call them
> survival programs, meaning survival pending revolution. We say
> that the survival program of the Black Panther Party is like the
> survival kit of a sailor stranded on a raft. It helps him to sustain
> himself until he can get completely out of that situation . . .

The intent of the Free Food Program is to supplement the groceries of Black and poor people until economic conditions allow them to purchase good food at reasonable prices.

The Free Food Program provides two basic services to the community:

Community members receiving bags of food from the Black Panther Party's Free Food Program, ca. 1972. Location, names, and photographer unknown.

1) An ongoing supply of food to meet their daily needs
2) Periodic mass distributions of food to reach a larger segment of the community than can be serviced from the ongoing supply

The community is provided with bags of fresh food containing items such as eggs, canned fruits and vegetables, chickens, milk, potatoes, rice, bread, cereal, and so forth. A minimum of a week's supply of food is included in each bag.

The Free Food Program requires a number of facilities and equipment. A building or warehouse or other facility is required from which to distribute the food on an ongoing basis. For the periodic mass distributions, trucks or large vans are needed. Depending on the number of people to be serviced, one or more buildings will be needed for storing the food. Refrigerators are required to prevent spoiling of meat and other perishable items. At least two cars or other vehicles must be available to transport those persons responsible for the procurement of the food. Finally, an office or communications center must be set up from which information about the program may be disseminated and questions about its services may be answered.

Community Workers' Day celebration, Arroyo Viejo Park, Oakland, California, July 22, 1972. Names unknown. Photo by Hank Lebo.

A minimum of six people is required to coordinate the Free Food Program. In order to cover as wide an area as possible, two people are responsible for the procurement of the food. The program depends almost entirely on donations of grocery store owners and wholesale food dealers. Once a collective decision is made as to how many people the program will service on an ongoing basis and how many will be serviced in the periodic mass distributions, procurement personnel will determine what food items must be purchased and in what quantity. They will need to visit as many grocery store managers or owners as possible, explain the purpose of the Free Food Program, and show the managers how their contributions will benefit the overall survival of the community. Procurement personnel may wish to concentrate on getting one specific food item from an individual manager or they may choose to get many items in the greatest number possible.

Two people must coordinate the transport and storage of the food until it is distributed. They will have to rely on community help in securing trucks and other vans in which to transport the food, and warehouses or other buildings in which to store the food. Churches are often very willing to make space available for food storage and also for distribution of the food. Personnel working in this area of the program must visit a number of people in the community in order to secure the needed facilities and equipment for transportation and storage.

Publicity is key to the success of the program, both in its ongoing aspect and for the mass intensive publicity campaign. Flyers must be distributed in large numbers throughout the community in a variety of places such as churches, schools and colleges, grocery stores, at sports events, and so forth. Posters should be placed in areas where a maximum number of people will see them. Radio advertising time, especially on Black-oriented stations, must be purchased. It may be possible to obtain this time free of charge by having such information advertised as part of the station's public service announcements. Newspapers should be contacted about doing one or more articles on the program. Publicity personnel may wish to speak at various community meetings or at church services in order to explain the program.

Even though most of the food may be secured free of charge, it will still be necessary to raise funds for printing of posters, flyers, radio advertisements, and any rental of facilities necessary. At least one person must coordinate fundraising and assume the primary responsibility for determining how much money will be needed for operating expenses and then allocating the money.

A secretary must be available in the office to handle all requests for food and to answer the community's questions concerning the program. The secretary must keep an accurate record of requests made so that the procurement personnel will have a clear idea of how much food is needed by the particular community being serviced.

Funds are secured from grocery store owners or managers and other businessmen; churches; social clubs such as fraternities or sororities; college or high school student organizations; and from on-the-street donation drives. The persons responsible for procurement of money must develop close contacts with all such organizations, with particular emphasis on community leaders who will hopefully be able to convince the community at large of the importance of the program. Once organizations decide that they wish to make financial contributions to the program, they may develop a variety of ways to raise the money such as a church bake sale or a student union dance. The persons handling fund-raising should also make suggestions to the organizations on how they could raise money.

Community personnel become involved in the program through the organizing efforts of the Free Food Program's staff. The staff succeeds in getting the community to really run the Free Food Program by requesting community persons to donate the use of their cars or other vehicles for transportation; asking them to work as drivers of these vehicles; seeking ideas for fund-raising from them and working with them on a consistent basis to raise the funds; getting them to distribute flyers and other publicity materials; and most important, securing their help in the actual distribution of the food. At first, people may doubt that it is possible for them to receive free food, but once they see the seriousness of the program, they will want to participate in order for the program to be successful.

Point Three of the Ten-Point Program of the Black Panther Party states: "We want an end to the robbery by the capitalists of our Black and oppressed communities." This robbery is clearly pronounced in the ridiculously high prices that we must pay for food, which is necessary for our daily sustenance. That is why everyone in the community, particularly those who are the poorest and most oppressed, can have their consciousness raised through the Free Food Program. The community begins to organize in protest against food stores that exploit them and in fact may even boycott these stores until their prices conform to what the community can afford to pay. Those who own and manage the stores will seek to lower their prices in order to maintain their business in the community and as a result will become unified with the people in the fight against economic exploitation.

Black Student Alliance

The Black Student Alliance in the Bay Area, founded in May 1972, grew out of a transitional period on the campuses across the country during which the rhetoric and flamboyance of the Black student movement gave way to the need for more concrete work to meet the practical needs of the students.

There had previously been calls for unity between the Black community and Black students, but there was still alienation between the two as well as a serious lack of communication and unity among Black students themselves.

With these conditions in mind, several Black student unions in the Bay Area pulled together to form the Black Student Alliance with the goal of creating concrete programs on the campus that would unify the student body and Black students with the Black community.

The programs devised fall under two broad categories—those necessary for the students' basic survival, and those required for a high quality of education. Survival programs include financial aid, child care, food, and transportation. Educational needs include relevant courses, progressive attitudes of instructors, fieldwork, and books and supplies.

In order to make Bay Area colleges better serve and be more responsible to the surrounding poor and oppressed communities, the Black Student Alliance has instituted a program for free books and supplies; a free transportation program; child care services; a financial aid program; a food program serving good, nutritious food at reasonable prices; and the initiation of relevant courses along with the demand for better instructors.

The alliance has also created and become involved in numerous programs in the community such as sickle-cell anemia testing; tuberculosis testing; free health clinics; the Seniors Against a Fearful Environment (SAFE) Program of the Black Panther Party; a shoe factory; and local election work.

Funds for the alliance's programs come primarily from the schools, student government, individual and organizational donations, and various fundraising benefits.

As the students and community work together to achieve community control of college boards, they can unite in demanding significant input and participation in the decision-making processes of the schools and at the same time make the schools more relevant to the community.

I. What programs can unify students?
    A. Needs of Black students for basic survival
        1. Financial aid
        2. Child care
        3. Lunch or dinner
        4. Transportation
    B. Needs of students in education
        1. Relevant courses
        2. Attitudes of instructors
        3. Fieldwork
        4. Books and supplies
    C. Some programs enacted in the alliance
        1. The fight for financial aid
        2. The fight for child care
        3. The fight for better food at cheaper prices
        4. The free transportation program
        5. Constant struggle for relevant courses and better instructors; initiation of courses
        6. Free books and supplies program
    D. Ultimately making schools serve and be responsible to the surrounding poor and oppressed communities
II. Unifying students with the community
    A. History of relationships between Black students and the Black community
        1. In the South, North, and West
        2. Difference between two-year colleges, four-year colleges, private and public
    B. Working in survival programs
        1. Health programs

        a. Sickle-cell anemia testing

        b. Tuberculosis testing

        c. Students working in free health clinics

    2. SAFE Program

    3. Shoe factory

  C. Working in local elections

III. Strengthening programs

  A. Funds from the schools, student governments

  B. Eventual community control of school boards

    1. In the process of achieving community control of neighborhood schools, students and the nearby community can unite in demanding real input and participation in the decision-making process

Landbanking

andbanking refers to the community entering the real estate market, buying land by direct purchase or often with borrowed money, and the leasing or occasional selling of sites for development. Therefore, employing the landbanking technique allows greater community control of the use and development of its land.

The landbanking concept has traditionally been associated with the environmental movement in the United States and the environmentalists have traditionally bypassed or run head-on into contradiction with Black and poor urban communities. The primary reason for this is that the focus of the environmental movement has been outside the inner cities. The inner-city resident (due to the uncontrolled growth and overdevelopment of the inner city) must focus on much more immediate aspects of survival first, including employment, housing, education (and facilities), food, clothing, and other basic necessities. He has little time to contemplate the beauty or necessity of "open space" or more parks. Thus, the ghetto dweller of the inner city sees the environmental movement as a luxury he cannot afford.

Thus far, attempts to find a practical approach to the common ground that Black and poor urban dwellers and environmentalists share have failed. Why? Environmentalists generally have failed to acknowledge or recognize the more immediate problems with which an urban dweller must contend. On the other hand, urban dwellers have failed to see the possibilities for the development of more urban open space (parks, recreation centers, etc.) as a source, not only of beauty, but also of employment, job development, a better environment for the rearing of children, and so forth.

In short, we must see a merger of land conservation and "human conservation"—the interconnection between the preservation of our natural and human resources, recognizing that each have little without the other.

In large urban areas, Blacks and other minorities are rapidly becoming the majority in overcrowded, blighted inner cities. Unemployment continues to spiral upward, further continuing the vicious cycle that locks generation after generation in slums and ghettos. The inner-city governments are controlled and run by business interests whose only concern for further "development" is geared primarily by a profit motive. Job development, improved education, and better housing for inner-city dwellers are not priorities, much less "open space" and more inner-city park facilities.

As mentioned before, landbanking as a concept has previously been developed and applied in suburban and rural areas. How, then, do we develop a concept of "urban landbanking" suitable to the needs of the urban dweller?

First, where's the land? In a crowded inner city, where does one find or create open space? The immediate and most obvious answer is perhaps seldom considered or seen for its potential use—the blighted, unsightly vacant lots that dot our cities. These lots can be acquired from their absentee landlords and developed into much-needed miniparks, tot lots, community gardens, and cultural or recreation centers. This provides future job development possibilities as well.

How?

If the city government structures have given open space and parks development such a low priority, and the urban dweller is locked in a bitter struggle of survival for the most basic necessities, how can this be done? By the effective merger of the environmental movement and the Black and poor of the inner cities.

The expertise and technical skill of the environmentalists, who have been implementing the landbanking concept so far, and the community organizations, groups, and individuals who wish to improve the quality of their lives, can be "the number," the winning combination in a struggle to not only preserve life but also improve the environment in which all live.

With this combination, the local structure can be used where it is advantageous, and where it is a hindrance, it can simply be bypassed. The local community at the grassroots level will be able to determine its desires and needs and see them fulfilled through such projects.

People's Free Employment Program

A People's Free Employment Program is obviously of no cost to the persons who make use of it. It is an especially needed service in the urban center where the Black and poor people seeking employment are usually shuttled from state office to state office between miles of red tape, where too few jobs are available and those few are often meaningless and degrading. Usually, the only alternative is a private employment agency, which charges a basic rate to locate a job for a person and, if a job is found, takes a commission or percentage of the person's salary for a period of time.

A People's Free Employment Program, then, is not only free but must avoid the bureaucratic approach to people. It must reflect sincere involvement in finding decent jobs for people.

If these basic things are done, any People's Free Employment Program will have more applicants than it can handle.

How to Set up the Program

I.   A central office facility is needed where employees and people who seek jobs can come or call.

II. A minimum of one person is needed to man the office, but more may be needed depending on the scale of the operation. A few volunteers or part-time staff who go out into the community to look for job openings is essential.

III. Develop a job information network.
     (Note: It is important to find out as much as you can about the job, the potential employer, etc. before you give someone information about the job possibility.)

A. The usual channels—obtain listings from state and local government agencies as well as school districts. These places regularly list—through public bulletins—jobs and job opportunities available

B. Newspaper ads—check newspaper ads for jobs available

C. Private business—call local factories, businesses, etc., to inquire about immediate and future job opportunities. Keep in contact with these people and build a relationship where possible

D. The "grapevine"—last, but very important. Friends, neighbors, friends of friends—anybody can know about a job opening. This is an important source that should not be overlooked

When you have accumulated any amount of information about job opportunities or possibilities, you should set up a file of your listings. This should contain as much information as possible about each job; these files must be constantly updated

IV. The importance of "keeping in touch."

A. You should maintain contact not only with possible sources of job information, but also with persons who come to you for help. Even if you are unable to help a person on the spot, you may find something of interest to him or her later. Set up a file of everyone who comes to you for help with information about their skills and interests. (You may find a job training program.)

Everyone has a right to a job, not only to guarantee survival, but to give a decent standard of living. Government and big business have failed to give this right and have failed to let us live as human beings. Based on this philosophy, a People's Free Employment Program helps people see that alternative structures can be established by the community, which will provide for its survival.

Register to Vote

Intercommunal News Service

The *Black Panther* is the official organ of the Black Panther Party. It is a tabloid-size newspaper that has published regularly every week since April 25, 1967. It is copyrighted by Huey P. Newton, is currently twenty-four pages, and is distributed nationally.

The Black Panther provides news and information about the work of the Black Panther Party chapters throughout the country; news and news analysis of the Black and other oppressed communities in the United States, Africa, and around the world; theoretical writings of party ideologists; and general news features on all matters relative to the liberation of humankind from oppression of any kind.

The Black Panther also provides service and survival information of every variety, such as guides including addresses and telephone numbers for city services as well as free services available.

The first issue of *The Black Panther* and several subsequent issues were produced with a typewriter, a mimeograph machine, stencils, and a stapling machine. The front-page story concerned the murder of a Black youth in the Richmond, California, community by a policeman and the action organized by the Black Panther Party to secure justice for the family of the youth.

Minimum equipment includes general office machines, a photo-offset Compugraphic typesetting machine, layout equipment, photographic equipment including a half-tone camera, and addressograph equipment.

The core staff of *The Black Panther* consists of members of the Black Panther Party for whom production of *The Black Panther* is one of several assigned duties within the party. The staff includes nonparty members who contribute their time and skills to the production of the paper.

The staff of twenty-five consists of four sections: editorial, including reporting, writing, editing and proofreading; layout, including typesetting, art and design; photo, including photo reporters and photo production; and distribution.

No Paid Ads

The Black Panther does not accept paid advertising or classified ads. It depends on sales, subscriptions, and contributions for operating funds. Ads that appear in *The Black Panther* recognize regular contributions of goods or services to the survival programs of the Black Panther Party and the community.

Funds are accumulated through direct sales on the streets in the community, the sale of the paper in community shops, shopping malls, barber shops, bars, and other centers where the people of the community gather, and in dispensing machines containing *The Black Panther* at highly traveled locations throughout the community.

Throughout the country each chapter of the party distributes *The Black Panther* in accordance with the needs and possibilities of its community. The paper is also sold by progressive bookshops and through a direct relationship with Central Distribution in Oakland in those cities that may not have a chapter of the party.

Members of the community are involved in the weekly production of the paper in different capacities on a volunteer basis including office work, reporting, photographing, writing articles, and distribution. In addition, both individuals and other community organizations are involved through the submission of information concerning their work in the community toward the objectives of survival and liberation.

The Black Panther is one of the chief consciousness-raising tools of the Black Panther Party.

1. The publishing of news and information from the Black and oppressed communities, which is generally ignored by the establishment press, exposes the true nature of that media as a tool of those responsible for the oppression.
2. The truthful presentation of news and information about Black and oppressed peoples, which is distorted and misrepresented blatantly in the establishment press, exposes the failure of that press and media to report honestly or fully on matters concerning Black and oppressed peoples.

Huey P. Newton being greeted by Chow En-Lai, Beijing, China, 1971. Other name and photographer unknown.

3. The consistent reporting of all news and information relevant to the interests of Black people, workers, oppressed peoples, youth, and the aged provides readers with a built-in interpretation of the news that is in their interests and consequently raises their understanding of the nature and condition of our society.

The Black Panther encourages individuals in the community to report to the newspaper either in person or by letter individual acts of repression, police brutality, or injustice. The paper acts as an important source of work for the legal aid survival program of the party, resulting in the involvement of the individual or individuals in the development of their defense.

Members of the community, particularly small businesses, are involved by stocking the paper at their place of business. Youngsters in

Elaine Brown with United Farm Workers organizers. Location and date unknown.
Photo by Lauryn Williams.

the community are involved in the street sales of the paper as a source
of pocket money for them.

4. Consistent coverage of liberation news from Africa, Latin America,
and southeast Asia from the point of view of the struggle of the
masses against U.S. and Western imperialism increases the
understanding of the reader of their oneness with the oppressed
of the world and strengthens the reader's resolve to intensify his
or her efforts toward freedom.

5. Interpretations and analyses of sports and entertainment news and
events from the point of view of liberation, the effects of racism, big
business, and the corruption of culture, increase the understanding of
the reader of the nature of our society.

I. NEWS

News is *now* information. A newspaper's primary job is to provide its readers with *now* information. For the Black Panther Intercommunal News Service (BPINS), *now* information means information affecting the lives of Black and poor oppressed peoples. For the BPINS, *now* information covers the period (week) between deadlines.

Now information consists of:

A. Facts about a happening or series of happenings

B. The source of those facts

C. Direct quotes or other verification of the facts when possible

II. THE NEWS ARTICLE (STORY)

The news article's *primary* purpose is to inform. Its secondary purpose is to interpret that information. The BPINS news article informs and interprets events affecting the lives of Black and other oppressed peoples.

A. news article consists of:

   1. *Now* information

   2. Background information—related facts earlier in time

   3. Interpretation. There are two ways to interpret events in a news article: 1) By the choice of and relative importance given to the facts (implicit interpretation); and 2) Clearly stated interpretation (explicit interpretation). The BPINS news article always contains a People's Party interpretation of the happening or event reported, both implicit and explicit.

III. WRITING THE NEWS ARTICLE

News writing must *above all else* be clear and precise. The language used must always be easy to read and uncomplicated. *Short sentences are the best sentences.* This is of primary importance for the BPINS.

> Forge simple words that even the children
> can understand;
> Words which will enter every house
> Like the wind
> and fall like red hot embers
> On our people's souls.
>
> Jose Rebelo, FRELIMO

A news article moves from the specific to the general; from the important to the less important; from the statement of the facts to the explicit interpretation.

The source of information contained in a news story must always be stated early in the article. There are several possible sources:

1. The reporter on the scene
2. BPINS sources
3. Official spokesman or official announcements
4. Witnesses to the event
5. Other media reports
6. "Sources"

IV. EDITORIAL WRITING

Editorial writing's *primary* purpose is to present a point of view on a happening or circumstance. The BPINS editorial writing is *always* in line with the Black Panther Party's fundamental position of "Service to the People," and "All Power to the People."

Editorial writing appears in the following forms in the paper:

1. The editorial
2. Columns
3. Special articles by party members
4. Review of books, films, or other cultural presentations
5. Cartoons

In the BPINS, our editorial position is always reflected in every article, feature, or column in the paper, with the possible exception of letters to the editor, signed commentary we print in order to refute, and ads.

V. THE FEATURE ARTICLE

Feature articles are general information articles meant to inform, educate, and/or entertain. For the BPINS, feature articles primarily educate (and we hope entertain) the reader in line with the program of the Black Panther Party.

Feature articles differ basically from news articles in two ways:

1. The *now* factor is secondary to the subject
2. The method of presentation is freer; however, the clarity and consciousness of the news article must also characterize the feature article

VI. PHOTO AND ARTWORK

The primary purpose of photo and artwork is to capture the attention of the reader and heighten the interest, curiosity, and entertainment of the reader.

Artwork includes layout (of pages, ads, etc.), section headings, copy dividers, and miscellaneous art bits or fun features.

VII. FUN FEATURES

Fun features are weekly items meant primarily to entertain the reader. BPINS fun features must educate as well as entertain the reader.

Fun features include puzzles, comic strips, word games, crosswords, and so forth. The entire staff must give thought to creative ideas for fun features especially suited to the aims and objectives of the BPINS.

People's Cooperative Housing Program

The People's Cooperative Housing Program is designed to provide decent, quality housing for low-income community residents. Federal and local government aid is certainly a requirement in order to implement this program, and in many cases strong community agitation and organizing will be needed to press city officials to fulfill their legal obligations.

The prime example for the implementation of a People's Cooperative Housing Program is the case of the City Center Replacement Housing Program in the city of Oakland. Insofar as many factors—legal obligation, local government reluctance, and urban renewal—came into play in the initial history of this program and insofar as these variables are common in many large metropolitan urban areas, a background on the struggle to force the city of Oakland to adopt a program of this type follows.

For the past decade, the city of Oakland sought to construct a large city center project in the heart of the downtown business district. A combination of business offices, small shops, department stores and the like, the project, together with the construction of interconnecting highways, would be a major endeavor for the city and was theorized to provide a substantial uplift for local business.

Making its initial headway in the fall of 1972, the construction of the city center project demanded the tearing down of approximately fifteen blocks of the downtown area, forcing the residents to relocate.

However, a little-used section of the Federal Housing Act of 1949 requires the construction of decent, quality replacement housing for urban renewal projects in those instances when there is not an adequate supply of low-income housing throughout the city. Specifically, federal law demands that replacement housing be constructed when the citywide vacancy rate is less than 5 percent.

On May 23, 1973, attorneys for the Black Panther Party and the East Bay

Legislative Council of Senior Citizens informed the Oakland City Council that, in fact, the city had less than a 5 percent vacancy rate and was therefore legally obligated to provide replacement housing in order to proceed with the city center project. Stunned, the council set up a citizens' committee to work along with the city's redevelopment agency to develop an adequate housing program.

Nearly a year went by before the city council finally took action. In the intervening months, the city asked the federal government to release it from its obligations. The government refused. In September 1973, the city council sent the citizens' committee proposal to "workshop sessions" hoping to kill or stall their recommendations there.

Finally, threatened with a long and costly litigation that might halt the construction of the city center project for years, the city of Oakland took action.

The result of the citizens' committee meetings, passed unanimously by the city council, was an unprecedented replacement housing proposal. The historic $12 million housing package provides for the construction of three hundred good quality housing units at an approximate cost of twenty-two thousand dollars per unit to be financed through a tax increment plan of six hundred thousand dollars annually.

Another unique feature of the package is that a nonprofit corporation, wholly controlled by community groups, will retain collective ownership and policy-making control over the entire housing complex. Rentals will not exceed 25 percent of the monthly income of the tenants, and a tenants' union will be established that will be open to membership for all tenants.

People interested in initiating cooperative housing programs should certainly enlist the aid of a lawyer or other persons familiar with local and federal housing laws. Community organizing will also certainly be necessary, in view of the reluctance of city officials to implement these laws in the people's interest.

Child Development Center

In the two years since the Child Development Center began, the staff working with the children have had the unique opportunity of observing children in their early stages of development in a communal lifestyle, and they have been very conscious of the profound effects it has had on the children's development.

Because of the racism that is prevalent in American society, there has been no previous study of the Black child's development at what is termed the "preschool age" and younger. And because communalism is the opposite paragon of the American family, there are no resources to study the development of children in a communal lifestyle.

We have developed a functional, comprehensive program that is divided into two categories: infant stimulation (for children from birth until one year) and sensorimotor development (one until two and a half years). Along with the infant stimulation program it was necessary to create our own developmental schedule. This would give us an accurate evaluation of the child to use as a guide to cultivate the child's developmental needs.

Development Schedule

Each child will be formally observed and evaluated, using the developmental schedule as a guide to determine in what areas development should be advanced, then an intensive stimulation program geared to each child's particular need will be conducted. A new evaluation will be made monthly.

The second category is sensorimotor development, which focuses on developing skills in knowledge of body parts and the interrelation between them; space and direction; body movement; rhythm; and primary skills.

The development schedule includes:

I. Motor skills
    A. gross (sitting up, crawling, clapping hands)
    B. fine (picking up small objects with thumb and forefinger, feeding oneself, changing toys from one hand to the other)

II. Adoptive (problem solving)
    A. ability to discriminate his bottle, familiar faces, missing objects
    B. make connections between similar objects

III. Verbalization
    A. chuckles, coos
    B. vocal and social response
    C. mono- and polysyllable words

IV. Self-awareness and responsiveness
    A. aware of strange situations
    B. smiles at mirror image
    C. responds to own name

These are just a few of the examples included in the four areas of development.

Sensorimotor Skills Curriculum

GROUP I

While the children are in this group it will be a transition period for them instead of following a set lesson plan. They will continue with their individualized stimulation program while adjusting to the "toddlers' schedule" and activities. When they have adapted to their new environment and are comfortable in it they will move on to Group II.

GROUP II

I. Sensorimotor skills
    A. Learning body parts
        1. Parts of the face
        2. Appendages: legs, feet, toes, arms, hands, fingers
    B. Space and direction
        1. Up and down

2. Here and there

3. Symmetrical activities, left and right

C. Basic body movement

   1. Eye and hand coordination

      a. Learning to make designs using a variety of media such as pencils, chalk, pastes, watercolors, finger paint, molding, and clay

   2. Eye and foot coordination

      a. Learning to walk in given directions

      b. Exercises in balance control

D. Rhythm

   1. Basic locomotor movement (done to music)

      a. Walking fast and slow

      b. Taking small and large steps

      c. Marching

      d. Jumping and hopping

E. Fine muscle development

   1. Hand dexterity and muscle control

      a. Individual finger strength

      b. Finger coordination

GROUP III

I. Sensorimotor skills

   A. Learning the interrelation between body parts

   B. Space and direction

   C. Basic body movement

      1. Eye and hand coordination

      2. Eye and foot coordination

   D. Symmetrical activities

   E. Rhythm

      1. Basic locomotor movement

   F. Fine muscle development

II. People's health

   A. Personal hygiene

      1. Washing hands

      2. Bathing themselves

      3. Brushing their teeth

III. Political education

IV. On practice

    A. Learning about their clothing and shoes, how to take them off and put them on

    B. Cleaning up after play and work

GROUP IV

Their program will be consistent with that of Group I of the Intercommunal Youth Institute's Curriculum, with the major emphasis on:

I. Primary skills

    A. Language arts

        1. Sound and sight recognition of the letters of their name

        2. Recognition of common shapes: line, circles, triangles, squares

        3. Ability to draw some of these shapes

        4. Recognition of common household and farm animals and plants

        5. Recognition of basic colors in the primary group

    B. Math

        1. Learn to count from one to ten

        2. Recognition of numbers one through ten

        3. Learning basic denominations of money

II. Physical education

    A. Games will be devised that:

        1. Promote cooperation among comrades

        2. Improve agility and finger dexterity

        3. Teach recognition of basic directions: backward, forward, etc.

III. Political education

    A. Personal hygiene and how it relates to staying well

IV. Political education

V. On practice

    A. Use of the telephone: dialing and speaking

    B. Care of clothing

    C. Cleaning after play and work

    D. Grocery shopping

    E. Table setting

    F. Making beds

VI. Vocalization

    A. Phonics

        1. Recognition by sound and sight

TODDLERS' SCHEDULE AND GROUPING:

7:30	Breakfast
8:15–9:30	Bathed, dressed, hair combed
9:30–10:00	Potty time
9:30–9:40	Group I
9:40–9:50	Group II
10:15–11:00	Class Groups II and III

OUTSIDE GROUP I

11:15–11:30	Potty time Group I
11:15–11:30	Potty time Groups II and III
11:30–12:00	Lunch
12:00–12:15	Potty time all groups
12:30–1:30	Nap time
1:45–2:00	Potty time all groups
2:00–2:30	Sensorimotor activity
2:45–3:00	Potty time
3:00–4:45	Outside
5:00–5:30	Dinner
5:45–6:00	Potty time all groups
6:15–7:15	Free time and getting ready for bed
7:30	Bedtime

People's Free Shoe Program

The average cost of a decent pair of shoes now ranges between thirty and fifty dollars, with the shoes lasting from three to six months. To provide shoes for a family of four could cost in the neighborhood of four hundred dollars annually. Thus, the need is seen for an alternative to these outrageous prices.

The People's Free Shoe Program has a twofold purpose: one, to take care of a basic human need; and two, to organize people to expand the program so they can have more control of their lives.

In starting a Free Shoe Program one should acquire some amount of storage space and a small office. The program can start out with just a few people doing the main thrust of the work. At this point it is very important to concentrate the work on becoming a nonprofit corporation. By having this nonprofit status, one can begin going to factories, wholesalers, and retailers for donations of excess shoes.

What happens is this: factories sometimes produce too many shoes of a certain type and have them in storage. As a nonprofit corporation, one can approach these factories for donations, which they can write off as a charitable contribution on their income taxes. The factory gets a tax deduction and the Free Shoe Program gets some shoes.

It is also very necessary, in the formative stages of the Free Shoe Program, to send out letters to corporations and smaller retail firms, keeping files on who will donate and how often. You should try to make as many personal visits as possible and follow up the visits with letters as the shoes begin to come in.

A group of people should be put together to distribute the shoes. They will have to learn measuring and have foot measurers, which can be acquired by donation from retail stores. At this point information should be distributed on a large scale to introduce the program to the community.

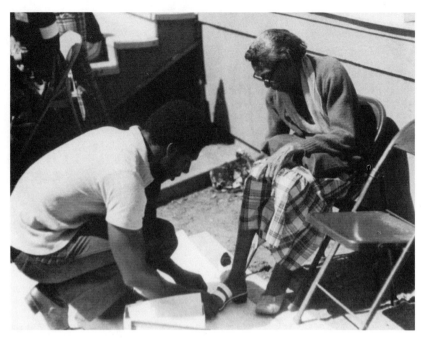

The Black Panther Party distributed shoes and clothing to the community, ca. 1972. Location, names, and photographer unknown.

As the program grows and develops, it will be seen that the donations for the large part will be lower quality shoes and there won't be enough to keep a very consistent program going.

Thus, having already organized a small group of people to work on the program, the next step is to organize a People's Shoe Factory.

One of the first things to involve people in is writing to foundations for initial funds to work with. The factory can be a benefit for brothers just getting out of prison who have been manufacturing shoes while incarcerated. They can be hired immediately by the factory, possibly giving some a chance for early parole. (When you write to foundations this is an important aspect to emphasize.)

The cost of running a shoe factory can be very high. Whatever funds are received should be spent wisely on the factory and not on administrative salaries. While some people are writing to foundations, other volunteers should be looking at the prices of leather from nearby tanneries or those outside the country. They should also be visiting other shoe factories to understand some of the basic formats of a shoe factory and what modifications will have to be made to start the People's Shoe Factory.

Another person should be responsible for finding someone who is very good in the lasting (sewing) operation and someone familiar with buttons. You should also seek people working in a shoe factory who can donate some of their time or become employees of the People's Shoe Factory for at least the first few months to work kinks out of the system. Quite a few people with these skills have been laid off. Also you should find someone familiar with the maintenance of the shoe machinery. Then another volunteer should begin finding people interested in designing shoes and begin organizing them as the designing department of the factory. It would be good to get some podiatrists and podiatric students involved in this department.

Still other volunteers should be looking into the best spots to locate the factory. There will be many vacant spots within the heart of the city to house the factory. It should have at least 4,500 square feet for efficiency and safety. These people should also price machinery needed, which can run as high as $12,000 to $13,000 used and $50,000 to $65,000 new. Good areas to keep tabs on are St. Louis, Los Angeles, and Boston. Boston alone has had more than sixty shoe factories move out in the past eleven years, leaving a great number of machines stored there that can be bought for dirt-cheap prices.

As things begin to fall in place, a group of people should be organized to keep the files straight. To keep the financial books straight you may be able to get an accountant or some accounting students to volunteer time. You can also send someone to school for accounting. Also law students and lawyers play a very important role in dealing with city ordinances regarding industry, such as zoning regulations. Also they will have to make sure the factory complies with federal regulations of the Occupational Health and Safety Act such as noise, heat, exposure to chemicals, and so forth.

The People's Shoe Factory should meet and surpass these standards anyway, regardless of the federal regulations, simply because it's a factory serving the community's interests, not profit. Therefore, extra time should be spent in designing the factory. There are architecture students, people who know plumbing, and other people with various skills who can be pulled together to make the factory conducive to working.

Once the factory is ready for production, you can start the purchase of leather for the upper part of the shoe; leather for inner and outer soles; glues and extra machine parts; threads; bells; packaging materials; and whatever else is needed.

A plan should have been laid out by then on how many and what kinds of shoes you plan to produce; how many people can be employed; and how much labor can be donated. Do you plan to have eating facilities? What is the maximum production potential of the factory? How much are the total expenses? How can money continue to come in to the program to cover expenses and expansion?

We will get into this question a little later, but first we'll look at what a People's Shoe Factory budget might look like.

Initial expenses

I. Price of machinery
II. Price for transporting machinery
III. Price of redesigning building
IV. Price for extra machine parts, etc.
V. Price for permits and other related expenses

Monthly expenses (excluding salaries)

I. Rent
II. Phone and water bills
III. Electricity
IV. Building upkeep and maintenance
    A. Cleaning equipment
    B. Repairing equipment
V. Price of raw materials
    A. Leather
    B. Packing materials
    C. Glue
    D. Heels and soles
    E. All other materials
VI. Machinery upkeep
VII. Cost of designing department
VIII. Cost of legal department and record keeping
IX. Cost of fund-raising department

X. Cost of distribution
    A. Truck and gas
    B. It may be necessary to open a storefront for distribution
XI. Cost of eating facilities (if provided)
XII. Miscellaneous

To get an idea of the type of funds we're talking about, let's look at the price of leather. If good quality leather is used (and it should be), it may run in the area of $1.25 per square foot in large bulk purchases. It takes around four square feet of leather to make a pair of men's shoes. Let's say you produced fifteen hundred pairs of shoes a month (most larger factories produce from two to three thousand pairs a day). The cost of leather alone per month would be seventy-five hundred dollars. If you add all the other expenses your monthly expenses could go as high as fifteen thousand dollars, not including salaries.

To be able to sustain this type of operation you will need more than foundation grants. One way the program could cut the cost is by selling some of the shoes. For instance, if the shoes being manufactured are in the thirty- to fifty-dollar bracket in retail value, it would be possible to sell these shoes at wholesale prices of twenty dollars a pair. If five hundred of your fifteen hundred shoes were sold it would leave one thousand for the program and ten thousand dollars per month. This will only partially help; the main thing that will be required is to pull from the various people ideas to keep the program going, because ultimately the Free Shoe Program belongs to the people.

People's Free Clothing Program

The Black Panther Party's People's Free Clothing Program provides new, stylish, and quality clothing free to the community. Black and poor people, especially children, often lack the necessary clothing to maintain good health. The People's Free Clothing Program is a means whereby people unable to buy decent clothing or lacking funds to buy good quality, stylish clothing can outfit themselves at no expense.

This program can be very beneficial to the community. For instance, if a person is looking for a job but has no good clothes to wear to interview for the job, the People's Free Clothing Program can be of great help. Dress and good grooming are very important to prospective employers. Thus, the People's Free Clothing Program may further aid the community's survival through the gaining of employment.

In addition, many Black children cannot attend school during the cold winter months because they don't have proper clothing. The People's Free Clothing Program can make it possible for them to attend school.

The minimum facilities required for this program are a clean storage place for the clothes until they are distributed; a sewing machine and other sewing equipment to make any necessary repairs; a building; and a truck, van, or other vehicle from which to distribute the clothes. Boxes or clothes bags may also be used during the distribution.

At least four people are needed for the efficient functioning of the People's Free Clothing Program. One person must be responsible for obtaining the clothing. If it is decided that clothes are to be distributed to five hundred men, women, and children, the person in charge of procurement must ensure that there are enough clothes for these five hundred people.

A second person must see to it that the clothes are properly stored before distribution and receive any needed repairs.

A third person is in charge of the distribution of the clothing. He or she must determine all the specifics as to when, where, and how the clothes will be distributed.

Finally, a fourth person must handle publicity, seeing to it that the community knows about the distribution of the clothing. This will involve obtaining as many free ads on radio, television, and in newspapers as possible, and mass distribution of flyers at churches, schools, colleges, and large community gatherings. It is vital to saturate the community with publicity so that people will know where to go on a regular basis to get clothing or the details of a single mass distribution.

Funds for maintenance of the program and the clothing itself are obtained through the solicitation of funds from a variety of sources.

The coordinator of procurement must visit various businesses, churches, etc., to ask for funds for the purchase of the clothing. Businesses especially like to have their names associated with such programs because it means, in fact, that they may get more trade from the community. Churches are usually willing to help in line with their practices and beliefs.

It may also be necessary to have a benefit concert or similar event in order to raise funds. A well-known entertainer or group will be asked to perform, hopefully free of charge, but at least for as low a fee as possible. The community will be charged a low, nominal fee for the benefit. Intensive publicity will also be needed for the success of this event.

Procurement

Procurement personnel will need to visit large department store chains in order to obtain good quality, stylish clothing. Many stores will sell their clothes at reduced prices when they are changing from one season's line to the next. Once the People's Free Clothing Program is thoroughly explained to them, they may even donate some clothing for free.

Community help is organized through visiting businesses, churches, schools, and other institutions. People will want to become involved in this program because most of them lack adequate clothing. They should see clearly how the program relates to their survival. It is important to effectively organize the community because their help is greatly needed in all aspects of the program. Program personnel may set up speaking engagements at various community gatherings to explain the program and ask for help.

Adequate clothing is key to man's survival, and therefore consciousness-raising through the People's Free Clothing Program is very important. By working together to obtain and distribute free clothing, the community becomes unified because it is working for the survival of all. The community comes to realize that it can work together effectively to correct one of its basic problems: the lack of good quality clothing.

Free Plumbing and Maintenance Program

The Free Plumbing and Maintenance Program provides a wide variety of services, including preventative maintenance care, plumbing repairs, and simple plumbing installations. The fixtures that require and receive the most attention are drains, water heaters, faucets, sinks, tubs, and toilets.

The minimum facilities needed to operate a functional plumbing and maintenance program are a telephone and storage area for tools. Essential equipment needed includes a car or truck, plumbing repair reference texts, plungers, and a large assortment of plumbing and general tools.

This effective program utilizes a minimum of four people. The coordinator establishes the time schedule, recruits volunteers, works on publicity, purchases tools and equipment, maintains inventory, and contacts stores and supply houses to obtain reduced prices. The plumber, in addition to routine plumbing and maintenance work, trains volunteers by conducting classes and on-site learning experiences. He also serves as a consultant to the experienced volunteers in the program. At least two volunteers, preferably from the community being served, go along on most jobs. They help carry out plumbing repairs and explain the survival programs to the people.

Funds to operate the program are generally donated by individuals, plumbers, and plumbing supply houses. University and foundation grants are also a major source of funding. The circulation of leaflets describing the program and the philosophy behind it, as well as participation in meetings of various organizations, constitutes important groundwork for raising funds.

Community people become involved in the program as a result of the publicity and the offer of a training program in plumbing repair for people who wish to increase their plumbing skills.

Out on a plumbing job, the "Each One Teach One" principle is employed. This consists of explaining to the customer the work being done and thus demystifying the process of repair.

The Free Plumbing and Maintenance Program is a vital community service. Not only is decent plumbing a human right, but denial of decent plumbing causes disease and deterioration of health. Unfortunately, high costs of plumbing supplies and labor effectively make decent plumbing available to only the rich in this country. People's plumbing programs, however, not only make decent plumbing available to everyone, but also involve the community in its own survival.

People's Free Pest Control Program

The People's Free Pest Control Program provides to the community free household extermination of rats, roaches, and other disease-carrying pests and rodents.

Particularly in urban areas where the majority of Black people live in crowded, rundown tenement housing, rats and pests are a serious problem. They frequently bite children and therefore should be eliminated for that reason alone.

In addition, rats further threaten human health by spreading such diseases as typhus fever, bubonic plague, food infestation, infectious jaundice, trichinosis, rat-bite fever, plus some twenty other known diseases. They also damage walls, pipes, doors, and foundations of buildings.

The People's Free Pest Control Program involves the basics of spraying homes and apartments and setting out necessary poisons. Every room, upstairs and downstairs, and the outside of entire buildings and individual homes are sprayed. Every effort is made to destroy the nesting and breeding places of harmful pests, and education is provided on how to starve pests.

To service a 3,500-unit housing project the following preparation materials and supplies are needed:

PEST CONTROL TECHNOLOGY
(Course, local college or university) $69.00
LICENSE APPLICATION FEE
(Required by State Structural Pest
    Control Board or agency) $50.00

EQUIPMENT

12 exterminator tanks—$60.00 each	$720.00
8 powder blowers	$29.32
4 six-inch extensions (two straight, two curved)	$8.00
12 pairs of gloves—$2.99 per pair	$35.88
6 respirators with goggles—$15.95 each	$95.70
6 respirators without goggles—$10.40 each	$62.40
1 pickup truck (new or used)	$3,800.00
12 uniforms—$12.00 each	$144.00

CHEMICALS: INSECTICIDE

Dursban—268 gal.—$20.10/gal.	$5,386.80
Vaponite 2—100 gal.—$15.50/gal.	$1,550.00
Diazinon 2D (dust)—50 lb. can ($25.00/can)	$25.00

CHEMICALS: RODENTICIDE*

200 lbs. est. pur.—$28.95 x 2 = $57.90	$800.00
TOTAL	**$12,776.10****

*It is difficult to estimate amounts of Rodenticide to be used. It will have to be purchased (at least one hundred pounds) and used over a period of at least three weeks to be able to make a reasonable estimate.

**These costs are based on the BPP Free Pest Control Program in Dallas, Texas.

In addition, an office with one or more telephone lines is needed from which to coordinate the program and handle requests for service. It may be required for those staff who perform the exterminating operation to obtain state exterminator's licenses. This will vary from state to state.

One van and pickup truck to transport the equipment must be on hand.

At least eight full-time people are required for the smooth functioning of the program. Four people perform the exterminating work. After securing all needed instructional materials, they are trained in the operation of the equipment and instructed in safety factors.

Two persons are primarily responsible for driving the van, pickup truck, or other vehicles used to carry the exterminating equipment. Two more persons handle office communications and must keep accurate records of all requests that are made for extermination services. It is particularly important that the date of the request be recorded so that community members do not wait long periods of time for service.

The communications staff may double as publicity coordinators. If housing projects, for example, are the major emphasis of the program, mass leafleting of the projects will need to be done in order to inform residents about the program.

To kick off the program the staff may wish to put on a demonstration of some kind. This would give the tenants an opportunity to see the process for themselves.

Funds for the maintenance of the People's Free Pest Control Program come from the usual variety of sources such as businessmen, churches, clubs, or other social groups. Individual businessmen should become familiar with the program, which can benefit many of them directly since they are often plagued by rats and roaches. Presentations at churches and at clubs should be made with the end goal of asking for financial contributions.

Since the tenants will be the major recipients of the service performed, small cash donations should be solicited from them if possible.

Widespread community personnel will be needed to run the program in all its aspects. A door-to-door campaign, if at all possible, is the best way to organize community help. Program personnel should visit individual tenants and give them a brief but thorough explanation of the program. If the tenants see the sincerity of the staff, the tenants will hopefully become enthusiastic about the program and volunteer their services.

The People's Free Pest Control Program was instituted by the Black Panther Party because of management's failure to provide the service to its tenants in public housing. We propose not to wait while we argue the point of who or what agency ought to provide the service. What is the community to do while the government and landlords make up their minds about the problem? By the community taking the initiative in establishing the program, it begins to question the inefficiency and unconcern of government and organizes to demand services by them. The program unifies the community by taking concrete action to sustain the people's daily lives.

The Black Panther Party's Ten-Point Program

March 29, 1972 Platform

What We Want, What We Believe

1. WE WANT FREEDOM. WE WANT THE POWER TO DETERMINE THE
    DESTINY OF OUR BLACK AND OPPRESSED COMMUNITIES.
    We believe that Black and oppressed people will not be free until
    we are able to determine our destinies in our own communities
    ourselves, by fully controlling all the institutions which exist in our
    communities.

2. WE WANT FULL EMPLOYMENT FOR OUR PEOPLE.
    We believe that the federal government is responsible and obligated
    to give every person employment or a guaranteed income. We
    believe that if the American businessmen will not give full
    employment, then the technology and means of production should
    be taken from the businessmen and placed in the community so
    that the people of the community can organize and employ all of its
    people and give a high standard of living.

3. WE WANT AN END TO THE ROBBERY BY THE CAPITALIST OF OUR
    BLACK AND OPPRESSED COMMUNITIES.
    We believe that this racist government has robbed us and now
    we are demanding the overdue debt of forty acres and two mules.
    Forty acres and two mules were promised one hundred years ago
    as restitution for slave labor and mass murder of Black people. We
    will accept the payment in currency, which will be distributed to
    our many communities. The American racist has taken part in the

slaughter of over fifty million Black people. Therefore, we feel this is a modest demand that we make.

4. WE WANT DECENT HOUSING, FIT FOR THE SHELTER OF HUMAN BEINGS.
We believe that if the landlords will not give decent housing to our Black and oppressed communities, then the housing and the land should be made into cooperatives so that the people in our communities, with government aid, can build and make decent housing for the people.

5. WE WANT EDUCATION FOR OUR PEOPLE THAT EXPOSES THE TRUE NATURE OF THIS DECADENT AMERICAN SOCIETY. WE WANT EDUCATION THAT TEACHES US OUR TRUE HISTORY AND OUR ROLE IN PRESENT-DAY SOCIETY.
We believe in an educational system that will give to our people a knowledge of self. If you do not have knowledge of yourself and your position in the society and the world, then you will have little chance to know anything else.

6. WE WANT COMPLETELY FREE HEALTH CARE FOR ALL BLACK AND OPPRESSED PEOPLE.
We believe that the government must provide, free of charge, for the people, health facilities that will not only treat our illnesses—most of which have come about as a result of our oppression—but that will also develop preventative medical programs to guarantee our future survival. We believe that mass health education and research programs must be developed to give Black and oppressed people access to advanced scientific and medical information, so we may provide ourselves with proper medical attention and care.

7. WE WANT AN IMMEDIATE END TO POLICE BRUTALITY AND MURDER OF BLACK PEOPLE, OTHER PEOPLE OF COLOR, AND ALL OPPRESSED PEOPLE INSIDE THE UNITED STATES.
We believe that the racist and fascist government of the United States uses its domestic enforcement agencies to carry out its program of oppression against Black people, other people of color, and poor people inside the United States. We believe it is our right,

therefore, to defend ourselves against such armed forces and that all Black and oppressed people should be armed for self-defense of our homes and communities against these fascist police forces.

8. WE WANT AN IMMEDIATE END TO ALL WARS OF AGGRESSION.
We believe that the various conflicts that exist around the world stem directly from the aggressive desires of the U.S. ruling circle and government to force its domination upon the oppressed people of the world. We believe that if the U.S. government or its lackeys do not cease these aggressive wars, it is the right of the people to defend themselves by any means necessary against their aggressors.

9. WE WANT FREEDOM FOR ALL BLACK AND POOR, OPPRESSED PEOPLE NOW HELD IN U.S. FEDERAL, STATE, COUNTY, CITY, AND MILITARY PRISONS AND JAILS. WE WANT TRIAL BY A JURY OF PEERS FOR ALL PERSONS CHARGED WITH SO-CALLED CRIMES UNDER THE LAWS OF THIS COUNTRY.
We believe that the many Black and poor, oppressed people now held in U.S. prisons and jails have not received fair and impartial trials under a racist and fascist judicial system and should be free from incarceration. We believe in the ultimate elimination of all wretched, inhuman penal institutions, because the masses of men and women imprisoned inside the United States or the U.S. military are the victims of oppressive conditions, which are the real cause of their imprisonment. We believe that when persons are brought to trial they must be guaranteed by the United States juries of their peers, attorneys of their choice, and freedom from imprisonment while awaiting trials.

10. WE WANT LAND, BREAD, HOUSING, EDUCATION, CLOTHING, JUSTICE, PEACE, AND PEOPLE'S COMMUNITY CONTROL OF MODERN TECHNOLOGY.
When, in the course of human events, it becomes necessary for one people to dissolve the political bands that have connected them with another, and to assume, among the powers of the earth, the separate and equal station to which the laws of nature and nature's God entitle them, a decent respect to the opinions of

mankind requires that they should declare the causes that impel them to the separation.

We hold these truths to be self-evident, that all men are created equal; that they are endowed by their Creator with certain unalienable rights; that among these are life, liberty, and the pursuit of happiness. That, to secure these rights, governments are instituted among men deriving their just powers from the consent of the governed; that, whenever any form of government becomes destructive of these ends, it is the right of the people to alter or to abolish it and to institute a new government, laying its foundation on such principles, and organizing its powers in such form, as to them shall seem most likely to effect their safety and happiness. Prudence, indeed, will dictate that governments long established should not be changed for light and transient causes; and, accordingly, all experience hath shown that mankind are more disposed to suffer, while evils are sufferable, than to right themselves by abolishing the forms to which they are accustomed. But, when a long train of abuses and usurpations, pursuing invariably the same object, evinces a design to reduce them under absolute despotism, it is their right, it is their duty, to throw off such government, and to provide new guards for their future security.

Legal Aid and Educational Program

Free Busing to Prisons Program

The Free Busing to Prisons Program maintains the bond between prisoners and their families by providing free transportation to (California) penal institutions. (It was later broadened into the Community Committee for Prisoners, Families, and Friends United. The Free Busing Program includes frequent trips to county jails, state penitentiaries, and other prisons.)

Initiated in southern California in 1970, the Free Busing Program first utilized rented buses, cars, and vans. Due to a massive increase in the number of Free Busing Program participants, a forty-passenger bus had to be acquired in 1972. The number of participants still exceeds the transportation available.

Trips to prisons are made on a regular, in most cases weekly, basis. A schedule comprising several weeks is made up in advance and circulated in the community. It is also published in *The Black Panther* and several local newspapers. Occasionally special arrangements are made at the community's request to take a trip to a prison that generally has few visitors.

The visitors gather at a central location, usually a party facility or church, before boarding the bus. The program also transports people from home to the bus and returns them afterward. Food is provided free of charge during the trip.

A major fund-raising drive is now underway to acquire monies with which to hire disadvantaged youth to work in the free busing program. The purpose is to help the youth learn an employable skill (driving and clerical skills).

Free Commissary for Prisoners Program

The Free Commissary for Prisoners Program is a community program designed to aid sisters and brothers confined in prisons throughout this country.

In the prison community the problem of survival is intense. In addition to being denied many of the basic necessities for day-to-day survival, prisoners must be on guard against constant physical attacks and abuse. Also, their mail is censored and they must pay for stationery, envelopes, and stamps. Prisoners who have no money are allowed only one free letter per week. Items such as warm underclothing, books, legal material, and other personal items must be purchased by the prisoners. Also, imprisoned women, who have largely been forgotten by the outside prison movement, have a great problem obtaining the items necessary for feminine hygiene (such as cosmetics and alternatives to lye-based soap).

Prisoners comprise a large and varied labor force for the state. The work they are forced to do includes the production of (in California) all state license plates, for which they earn from two to twenty-four cents an hour. With these exceedingly low "wages," prisoners must purchase items to satisfy their survival needs from a canteen or commissary at exploitative prices.

In addition, there is usually a surcharge or tax (10 percent in California prisons), which goes into an inmate's "welfare" fund, controlled by the prison administration.

Furthermore, prisoners must purchase their basic necessities only during the specific days on which they have commissary privileges.

The prisoners' right to live and function like human beings has been cruelly relegated to the level of "privileges" by the state. The basic human right to bathe, to have warm and adequate clothing, books, legal and other reading material, correspondence, and communication with the outside world are all vital to the survival of the oppressed prison community.

We cannot even begin to speak of freedom for all poor and oppressed people without acknowledging and in some concrete way dealing with the oppression faced by our incarcerated sisters and brothers.

The Free Commissary for Prisoners Program provides inmates with basic necessities such as toilet articles, clothes, and shoes. It also provides items requested by prisoners such as radios and record players. The items and funds are solicited from local businesses and the public.

The program consists of an intake system to receive prisoner requests for commissary items and a system to send out the articles. Prisoners generally make their needs and requests known through letters to someone who works with or knows of the program. The items are sent out by mail after they are bought or donated. The program attempts to get individuals and groups to sponsor prisoners by regularly obtaining commissary items for them. Copies of prison rules and regulations are obtained and consulted for information regarding prison rules that govern receipt of commissary.

Legal Aid for Prisoners Program

This program is maintained primarily through correspondence with prisoners—the sending and receiving of information needed to handle prisoners' legal matters and affairs. Where needed, a referral service to attorneys and other types of legal aid is provided.

Organizing a People's Campaign

I n the 1973 Oakland city elections, Bobby Seale and Elaine Brown conducted an astoundingly successful People's Campaign for the positions of mayor and city councilwoman. They ran on the Bobby Seale and Elaine Brown Fourteen-Point Program to Rebuild Oakland, a starting point from which not only Oakland but all cities throughout the country can begin to move and transform the current one-sided, negative, and essentially antipeople urban economy into one in which the city's priorities are directed toward the people rather than corporate interests. The following information relates to their campaign and the People's Program they introduced.

When a decision is made to run for office, it is usually a result of the frustrations of a community that has little or no input into or control of the local institutions of government (be it a school board, a city council, etc.). A People's Campaign will have two purposes—to educate its area residents about the issues and to win a seat or position that will increase the people's control in their community.

Many issues are put forward by aspirants to political office. But the problems candidates identify are often not the most important ones to the community, and the solutions they propose are many times vague and superficial.

The People's Candidate must have the true interests of the community at heart. His or her candidacy must be motivated by the people's concrete desires and needs, and by the program, a People's Program, the result of the community's actual ideas and suggestions. The people's platform must promise to improve the people's quality of life but at the same time be realistic, practical, and realizable.

The issues identified must be those gut ones that affect the daily lives of the people, which certain establishment candidates always promise to solve but never do. Unemployment, indecent housing, improper medical and child care, and poor quality education are but a few examples. In addition, the People's Candidates must address themselves to issues peculiar to their locales, which affect their constituency directly, aside from those that plague all oppressed communities.

After establishing that there is a base of support, the key is to know your area or community thoroughly.

What follows are some basic outlines of organizing methods and strategies used in the Oakland mayoral and councilmantic elections when the Black Panther Party ran two candidates, Bobby Seale and Elaine Brown, for office in a highly successful campaign in the spring of 1973. It should be understood, however, that these are only basic outlines and techniques. Each city or area will have differences. All of the methods may not work or be needed—practice will tell.

Breaking Down the City

One of the initial steps is to "break down" or map out the city or area you are trying to organize. For the Oakland election, the city was sectioned off into nine major areas (sections). The sections were determined by basic geographic, ethnic, and economic lines that have come to exist in the city. For example, Section 5 is basically a middle-income, Black, working-class community. Section 4 is basically a mixed ethnic area, where the bulk of the Oakland Chicano community lives. Each section was subdivided into subsections, and finally down to precincts (regular voting precincts as defined by the county) for organizing. Each division (section, subsection, precinct) had a coordinator. Each coordinator had specific responsibilities.

PRECINCT

    I. Precinct coordinator (each precinct may have between three and six hundred registered voters)

      A. Must become a voter registrar

      B. Must organize and coordinate ten or more precinct workers

      C. Must have time weekly to organize in an approximate ten-square-block area where you live

      D. Distribute leaflets, brochures, bumper stickers, posters, and other vital information to your precinct workers

      E. Call and chair precinct workers' meetings

F. Set up block meetings in homes with the candidates

G. Know and explain to precinct workers their designated areas of work within the precinct area

H. Acquire an assistant precinct coordinator who volunteers to do the same basic work along with you

I. Understand and be able to explain thoroughly to precinct workers how to work from voter registration sheets

J. Things a precinct coordinator and assistant precinct coordinator will need:

    1. Telephone date book

    2. Notebook, large size

    3. Map of precinct

    4. Briefcase

    5. Copies (four) of the voter rolls for your precinct

    6. Bumper stickers of candidates

    7. Posters of candidates

    8. Voter registrar books

II. Precinct worker

A. Become a voter registrar

B. Contact and keep sixty to one hundred registered voters informed about the campaign, with as much face-to-face contact as possible

C. Pass out all leaflets and brochures to all sixty to one hundred registered voters to whom you will be assigned by address

D. Things a precinct worker will need:

    1. Telephone date book

    2. Notebook

    3. Small briefcase

    4. Voter rolls sheet of the sixty to one hundred voters assigned

    5. Voter registrar book

In addition to these types of campaign work there are others:

I. Campaign office work

A. Helping with mailing lists, etc. Work consists of organizing names of contacts by address, city, and state. Envelopes have to be stamped and addressed.

B. Typing and filing consists of keeping various lists typed and filed properly. Letters have to be written. Records have to be kept and updated.

    C. Answering phones and taking messages: being sure information reaches the person it is intended for.

    D. Making phone contact consists of phoning people and informing them of certain things that are going on with the campaign, asking them to be at a certain place at a certain time for a particular reason, i.e., campaign meetings, dinners, etc.

II. Campaign fund-raising

    A. Organizing benefits consists of everything from phoning friends and asking them to give a party, to organizing large-scale entertainment affairs.

    B. Collecting funds consists of going door-to-door in a precinct and to businesses asking for donations to support the campaign.

III. Organizing groups and organizations

    A. Organizing churches consists of attending churches on Sunday and meeting the minister. You must also meet the congregation, shake their hands, and introduce yourself. Have information on the campaign.

    B. Organizing schools consists of making contact with campus organizations and getting them involved with the campaign to the point where the student body will become involved on different levels.

    C. Organizing small businesses into the campaign consists of talking to them about the issues and how our program will change their condition for the better.

IV. Voter registration

    A. Being a voter registrar consists of attending class for approximately one hour at the county registrar's office. The work entails carrying the voter registration book at all times possible, registering people who are not registered currently in the county.

Election Day

. . . is almost a separate organizing effort in itself.

Types and areas of work on election day

In each section:

I. Precinct worker
    A. Distributes door-hangers—4:00 a.m. starting time, last-minute
       material to get out the vote
    B. Poll watcher—functions as an observer at polls to see that election
       procedures are followed properly without any discrepancies
    C. Leaflet one hundred feet away from polls
    D. Get out the vote—start around 10:00 a.m. in certain precincts
       (door-to-door)
    E. Help decorate vans and cars that will be transporting the voters—
       starting at 6:00 a.m.
II. Maintain home as a satellite center for precinct workers in your
    section and subsection
    A. Make home open to the five to ten precinct workers in the
       subsection where you live
    B. Precinct workers would be stopping by throughout the day for
       coffee, to make phone calls
    C. Person remaining at the house would have to take telephone
       messages for precinct workers
    D. Van drivers would also be dropping by to call in and receive
       messages
III. Driver
    A. Take people to the polls
    B. If voters needing rides have children, the children are to ride in
       the van (station wagon, etc.) with you
    C. Children stay in van with driver while person votes
    D. Take voter (and children, if they have them) home. Check satellite
       center for new names from section or precinct coordinators
IV. Telephone caller at home
    A. Call everyone in your neighborhood and urge them to go out
       and vote. If they need a ride, call satellite home in your section
       with the name, address, phone, time, ride needed, and number of
       children if babysitting service is needed
V. Cooking
    A. For precinct workers
VI. Office work
    A. Receptionist, communications person, aids section leader in
       dispatch operation

B. Runner does necessary driving within section to
satellite centers, etc.

VII. Other

A. There's always something!

Seven-Point Revenue-Raising Plan

1. A 5 percent capital gains tax on the transfer of income property and property of large corporations. This progressive measure seeks to tap "capital gains"—the profits large businesses and corporations normally make upon their sale or in business transfers—not drive business away. $4.5 million can be raised in this way.

2. A 1 percent tax on intangible stocks and bonds (small home owners and the elderly are exempt). It is estimated that Oakland residents own $2.8 billion in stocks and bonds, concentrated in the hands of the rich and the super rich. This minimal 1 percent tax, with a basic seven-thousand-dollar exemption across the board, adds $10.5 million to available city funds.

3. Reinvestment of the city budget reserves and fund balances in banks that pay at least 6 percent interest rather than those paying the 5 percent the city now receives. The $20 million now known to be held in this way equals an additional two hundred thousand dollars if reinvested. Recently, research has uncovered more (upward of $50 million) stashed away in such "reserves." Oakland's rich banking firms certainly do not need to be subsidized, least of all by the poor.

4. An increase of fees at the two city-owned golf courses by 50 percent will bring in an additional $250,000 annually.

5. Increase the rental payments paid by the Oakland Coliseum owners, who can certainly afford it, to cover the $750,000 in construction bonds the Reading administration is currently paying.

6. A residency requirement for Oakland police and firemen, 72 percent of whom live outside Oakland, will bring more than $15 million back into the general economy of the city and approximately $1 million into the city budget itself.

7. A tax to be placed on so-called public utilities such as Southern Pacific Railroad and others would add up to at least five hundred thousand dollars annually, depending upon the tax rate imposed.

This all adds up to $17.7 million revenue raising funds, which, when combined with the $4.5 million in revenue sharing funds, equals a total of $22.2 million—more than one-quarter of the current city budget. These funds will be directly accessible for use in meeting our pressing city and community needs. In all, including the $14 million in additional funds from the imposition of the residency requirement, $36 million will flow within the general city economy, sparking a boom in both employment and business.

Funds from the revenue raising/revenue sharing plan will be used to implement and develop major community social service programs, along with financing certain vital city services. Two important areas of city services to be funded are:

Street lighting and street repair: $2 million annually will provide 1,500 to 2,000 blocks of well-lit streets for that quarter of our population residing in the high-crime areas.

Environmental protection: $2 million in funding can be used to safeguard Oakland's natural environment.

Major social programs to be funded include:

Preventative medical health care: $2 million will provide for eight mobile health care units and equip them with supplies and personnel to meet the health needs of those who cannot visit doctors regularly.

Child care: The present emergency needs for Oakland's preschool programs, children's centers, migrant farm day care, and campus day care will be adequately handled with $1 million in funds.

Seniors Against a Fearful Environment (SAFE): $2 million annually would provide for some one hundred radio-equipped passenger vans, employ more than three hundred people, and provide round-the-clock transport/escort services, reducing muggings by 70 percent. Presently, 33 percent of all crimes in Oakland are committed against our senior citizens. They deserve the best.

Education improvement: An expenditure of $2.2 million would guarantee that the 155 jobs within the Oakland school system are maintained. It would also begin to provide for much-needed textbooks, materials, and supplies our children need to grow and learn. Training programs for teachers' aides will also begin.

Economic development: $4 million in funding would finalize plans and lead to the construction of the proposed Multi-Ethnic International Trade and Cultural Center in Oakland.

Consumer protection: Protection from bad (perhaps even poisonous) foods and unnecessary increases in consumer prices by hiring and training Oakland residents in this field.

Elaine Brown, a People's Candidate in '75

PART II
Eliminate the Presidency

Black Panther Party Position Paper on the Elimination of the Offices of President and Vice President

T*he Black Panther Party Position Paper on the Elimination of the Offices of President and Vice President* was first published in February 1974, during the time the Senate Watergate Investigation Committee was conducting hearings on the Watergate scandal. Although the committee has discontinued its investigation, our proposal to eliminate the offices of the executive branch is no less timely; in fact its importance is now more apparent than ever. With the forced resignation of one chief executive, Richard M. Nixon, as a result of the exposure of some of his many crimes against the people, and his subsequent pardon for these crimes by his hand-chosen successor, Gerald Ford (whose action was described by one national leader as "the grossest miscarriage of justice in history"), the necessity increases for justice-minded Americans to take swift action toward abolishment of the corrupt executive offices, as the following proposal demands.

Introduction

A conspiratorial coup d'etat intended to secure for Richard M. Nixon the divine right of kings has been revealed through the hearings of the Senate Select Committee on Presidential Campaign Activities. This conspiracy undermines our country's republican form of government, jeopardizes our country's potential for good in the world, and constitutes a serious threat to peace and progress for all humankind.

The most dangerous aspect of this conspiracy is the wide-scale application of the principle of executive privilege as a means toward consolidation of power into the hands of the presidency. For the American people the result has been blatant violations of fundamental democratic rights, constant increases in the cost of living with massive increases in profits for the corporations, nation-wide reversals of limited gains for oppressed ethnic and minority Americans, a wholesale breakdown in services, and a dehumanized and spiritless society.

The expansion and consolidation of U.S. economic, political, and military force and power abroad has made the president of the United States more pow-erful than any king or tyrant in history. It has tricked the American people into becoming coconspirators with the U.S. empire builders and has compelled us to pay the bill through exorbitant taxation.

Secret Wars

Using the flower of our youth as cannon fodder, the U.S. empire builders have waged undeclared and secret wars of military aggression against peoples of the world struggling for self-determination; they have waged cartel and monop-oly wars of economic aggression against the demands of the peoples of the world for economic independence; they have waged diplomatic wars against the United Nations's attempts as peacemaker and world forum.

Watergate and its revelations have provided a dire warning to the American people: act now to halt this conspiracy and create safeguards against further such conspiracies, or face the imminent imposition of a police state at home and the wrath and condemnation of the freedom-loving peoples of the world!

The Proposal

We, therefore, call for the total elimination of the offices of the president and vice president of the United States of America and the return of all the powers usurped by these offices to the duly elected representatives of all the people, the Congress of the United States of America.

Radical restructuring in the executive branch of government, which reas-serts and makes manifest the power of the people consistent with the intent of the preamble to the U.S. Constitution and its Bill of Rights is the only path to the realization of the American dream.

Reforms of the existing practices will not safeguard the American people and ideals for which we strive from the coup-makers and Watergaters of a later age. They will only induce complacency and delay the inevitable confrontation.

The Historical Argument

Thomas Jefferson lived in a boardinghouse and walked to his inauguration; Richard Nixon has dressed a palace guard in nineteenth-century uniforms of royalty and has "Hail to the Chief" played each night at dinner. How did this regal mutation of "elected despots," as Jefferson called them, come about?

In 1776, the Founding Fathers drew on some two thousand years of recorded Western history to explain their "right of revolution" to the world. Their sources: the Greco-Roman, Judeo-Christian, Anglo-Saxon traditions.

The ideas of individual dignity, governmental accountability to the governed, and equal justice under law were time honored. What was new, unique, and revolutionary was the concept—the "checks and balances" of power—of how to implement the rhetoric that all people have an equal right to pursue life, liberty, and happiness. The framers of the American Revolution executed a stroke of genius: the executive, though not completely a figurehead, was to be checked systematically and without violence from becoming a king.

When King George III of England and his minister Lord North claimed the tyrannical vetoes and controls that we today call executive privilege, the great conservative Edmund Burke argued forcefully that it was not what some lawyer assured the king "he could do, but what humanity, reason, and justice tell him he ought to do." So the Congress was empowered to represent the ever-changing needs of the electorate and the courts to protect the individual from the ambitions of the executive.

Within a decade of the signing of the Declaration of Independence, the counterrevolution had begun. Ruling forces tried to use the Constitution to disenfranchise the masses of American people. Radical and conservative forces fought back after the army had put down a series of worker-farmer rebellions and managed to attach the Bill of Rights as a series of amendments to the Constitution. But from that time on, the executive branch has swollen, steadily usurping power from the courts. The kinglike executive has preempted the decision-making process inherent in the original checks and balances plan. The executive, by claiming to represent "all of the people," gets around representing any of the popular interests and instead becomes, inevitably, the captive of special interests. The last several decades have revealed the complete emergence of the royal executive.

The Moral Argument

We have called to these shores those forsaken in their native lands, saying to each and every one alike, this is your home: "Send these, the homeless, tempest-tossed to me . . ." It mattered not from what nation they came, nor of what faith, nor of what sex or physical capability. America reached out her arms and said, "Come, ye disconsolate," no one here shall disdain you or rule your life. Yes, America held a dream.

Through the years, America insisted her experiment was workable, her dream was feasible. We, wretched of the earth collected on these shores, could iron out the rough points if we clung to the idea of democracy: government by the people, of the people, for the people—all the people! No one group could come here and dictate over another, neither Jew over Gentile, nor Irish over Italian nor white over Black, nor man over woman. And, in our effort we not only established our laws but also created the method, the form of government by which our democratic ideals would be carried out to reflect our ethic: "One nation, under God . . . with liberty and justice for all."

The dream became twisted and distorted with our Blacks herded into ghettos; Native Americans onto wretched reservations; Mexicans and Puerto Ricans shuffled into barrios; poor whites forgotten among the "purple mountains' majesty"; Jews forced to deny their heritage; and Irish and Italian and Japanese and Chinese and all the others suffering their bitter spot upon the stage. Nevertheless, we still clung and tried to wrest the sweet from the bitter, and while each one in a separate cry proclaimed "nobody knows the trouble," each one began to try to understand the other.

With all of it we molded a tradition: the realization of our dream. For with all our differences we seemed and seem to agree about the character of America. From the barrios and the ghettos, from the southern mountains to the northern plains, from the universities to the streets, from the industrial plants and factories, from all corners, the voice of America screamed and insisted, "I have a right to live! That's what America means!"

Sacred Task

Ours, then, has become a sacred task. It is the collective task of the American people and future generations of Americans to shape and hone and refine this dream 'til it be real. It is not the charge of the part of us, but of the whole; not of one race, but of many; not of one party, but of all; not of one man, but of all.

We duly elect our representatives to Congress so the voices of America can be heard and our will be done.

We did not and do not ask one man to preside over our affairs or to shape our dream, but select many among us to perform the task. Who, then, is this president who wields a greater power than us all? Who is this man who dares challenge the very fiber of our dream to provide a government ruled by the governed? What privilege does this president carry that he dares to rule us, the people, as though by divine right? What monster have we created, who by turning the phrase "divine right" to "executive privilege" shall destroy a tradition that began in opposition to absolute despotism?

We could not have said that the life of every human being is important, to have allowed one man to commit murder sanctioned by "executive privilege." We did not mean to say that the property of every person must be respected, to then allow one man to burglarize in the name of "executive privilege." We did not mean that we would take our personal income as a tax to be centralized in the general public interest, only to have it used for the personal pleasure of one man because of his "executive privilege."

We, here and now, in this historic spot, have the opportunity to make such a change, for these are times to which witness can be born as to the ultimate evils of the presidency. Let us be unafraid to make change that neither defies tradition nor violates the law, but serves to benefit posterity in its wisdom. Let us be unafraid to meet the challenge laid before us by our founders, so long ago, to have such government that derives its "just powers from the consent of the governed."

The Legal Argument

It is not the intention here to interpret the Constitution of the United States of America, but to argue in the Constitution's own words that the intent of the Constitution regarding the president of the United States was to allow such limited power to that office as to make such a person in effect little more than a figurehead. The intent of the Constitution is to guarantee a republican form of government administered by the people, for the people, and through a representative Congress of the people. Further, the Constitution allows for the abolition and creation of laws as Congress deems necessary to provide flexibility in government to constantly serve the interests of the people in the historic course of human events and the growth and development of the country.

It cannot be argued that the U.S. Constitution does not provide for a president, for that is self-evident. However, the Constitution clearly does not allow the president powers that Congress does not deem necessary and proper. With this general theory in mind, the argument can be extended to our present historic place, which has revealed most recently in the Watergate affair the evils and potentially greater evils of necessity of a congressional act supporting Constitutional incumbent duties out of the hands of one man, without violating but rather enforcing the supreme law of the land:

1. The Constitution of the United States of America states in Article I, Section 8, that Congress shall have power to "make all laws which shall be necessary and proper for carrying into execution the foregoing powers, and all other powers vested by the Constitution in the government of the United States, or in any department or officer thereof."

2. The Constitution designates few powers to the president and none without some form of congressional consent. The first power of the president as outlined in the Constitution, under Article II, Section 2, provides that the president "shall be commander-in-chief of the Army and Navy of the United States, and of the militia of the several States." However, Article I, Section 8, grants the power to Congress only "to raise and support armies . . . to provide and maintain a navy," and "to provide for organizing, arming, and disciplining the militia, and for governing such part of them as may be employed in the service of the United States . . ."

3. The Constitution does not allow the president the power to administer any action carrying the weight of a policy decision under any such aegis as executive privilege. The very offices of the executive department are created by Congress, the heads of which are only nominated by the president: Article II, Section 2, of the Constitution says that the president "shall nominate, and by and with the advice of and consent of the Senate, shall appoint ambassadors, other public administrators and consuls, Judges of the Supreme Court, and all other officers of the United States, whose appointments are not herein otherwise provided for, and which shall be established by law . . ."

4. Besides outlining the limited powers of the president, the Constitution further provides safeguards against abuse of presidential authority. For example, not only is the president subject to impeachment from office, but he or she is also subject to punishment under the law while in office for violation of the law of the land and is not immune to such, as is applicable to any other citizen of the United States. Not only does Congress have the power to impeach a

president, but it also has the power to diminish or increase its own powers or the powers of the executive department or of any other department or branch of the government, which changes in law shall become the supreme law of the land: "This Constitution, and the laws of the United States which shall be made in pursuance thereof; and all treaties made, or which in every State shall be bound thereby, anything in the Constitution on laws of any State to the contrary notwithstanding." (Article VI)

Implementation of the Proposal

1. Whereas the Senate Select Committee on Presidential Campaign Activities had been given the task of formulating legislation for Congress that would have prevented or discouraged the repetition of those or similar acts as revealed to have been committed during the 1972 presidential election campaign, it is therefore fitting and proper that a similar Senate Select Committee consider the above proposal.

Consequently, the campaign will be launched with a dramatic press conference by a small group of distinguished Americans led by Huey P. Newton on the steps of the Senate Office Building in Washington, D.C., during the course of such hearings to submit our proposal to this Senate Select Committee.

2. The widest possible distribution and promotion of the position paper to all segments and groupings of the American people and the encouragement of the widest possible discussion and debate of the proposal from community to national levels.

3. The early creation of nonpartisan, community bodies and ad hoc committees of organizations, trade unions, and associations as advocates of the proposal. The encouragement of cosponsorship of the proposal by community organizations, trade unions, churches, and political parties locally, regionally, and nationally.

Long-Range Goals

1. The creation of regional coordinating committees to provide guidance and help to local community activities around the proposal.

2. The calling of a nonpartisan national organizing convention for the purpose of organizing national action on the proposal, with the aim of its adoption as a plank in the platforms of all political parties.

3. A massive national action in Washington, D.C., for implementation of the proposal and the creation of an executive of administrative experts answerable to the people through its elected representatives in the Congress of the United States of America.

PART III
People's Artists

Songs by Elaine Brown and
Poetry by Ericka Huggins

The music and poetry of the liberation struggle are a reflection of the innermost thoughts and emotions of an oppressed people as well as an expression of their culture. The revolutionary musician and poet seek to put the ideology of the struggle into an artistic form that the people can identify with. Music particularly is an important medium of expression and communication in the Black community. In the four centuries that Black people have been in America, music has been used to tell of the history of oppression and of the determined intent to end that oppression.

Sisters Elaine Brown, chief spokesperson for the Black Panther Party, and Ericka Huggins, director of the Intercommunal Youth Institute, songwriter/vocalist and poet, respectively, are skilled people's artists. Elaine's songs, all written by her, are, as she so often says, really written by the people because they reflect the joys, hopes, fears, and aspirations of the people. The sometimes sad but always inspirational ballads of Sister Elaine are the expression of a talented, sincere revolutionary. Equally beautiful and creative are Sister Ericka's poems. The refreshing style and pointed messages of her poetry speak out to people everywhere in a tone singular and universal.

"Until We're Free" is the statement of a revolutionary in words and song—words erupting out of the manifold experiences of struggle and song flowing out of the pain and suffering of Black life in America. These are love songs expressing Elaine Brown's deep and abiding sense of oneness with all oppressed humankind, her devotion to her comrades in battle, her faith in the victory that will be realized through the people's will, determination, and effort, love songs that touch and stir the heart. A consuming talent, a total dedication, and a proven commitment are combined in Elaine Brown, making her the first, genuine People's Artist America has produced.

Huey P. Newton

Elaine Brown's Statement on *Seize the Time*

In all societies, the way of life of the people, their culture, mores, customs, etc., evolve from the economic basis of that society. The United States is a capitalist society, the system of capitalism being one of exploitation of man by man, with byproducts such as racism, religious chauvinism, sexual chauvinism, and unnatural divisions among the people. In other words, it's a dog-eat-dog society. But it's not a dog-eat-dog world.

Men are not innately greedy, nor are they innately uncooperative with each other. Therefore, it is our goal, it is the goal of the Black Panther Party, and must be the goal of all men, to create conditions in which men can start being human, can begin to cooperate with each other, can love each other, in fact, in peace. Men cannot do this without an arena in which to do so. In other words, in an exploitative system men are forced to exploit. In an unkind system, men are forced to be unkind. In a world of inhumanity, men will be inhuman. In a society that is warmongering, men will war. These are the aspects or the way of life of a people who are part of a capitalist system.

And songs are a part of the culture of society. Art, in general, is that. Songs, like all art forms, are an expression of the feelings and thoughts, the desires and hopes, and so forth, of a people. They are no more than that. A song cannot change a situation, because a song does not live and breathe. People do.

And so the songs in this album are a statement—by, of, and for the people. All the people. A statement to say that we, the masses of people, have had a game run on us; a game that made us think that it was necessary for our survival to grab from each other, to take what we wanted as individuals from any other individuals or

Elaine Brown,
ca. 1972. Location
and photographer
unknown.

groups, or to exploit each other. And so, the statement is that some
of us have understood that it is absolutely essential for our survival
to do just the opposite. And that, in fact, we have always had the
power to do it. The power to determine our destinies as human
beings and not allow them to be determined by the few men who
now determine them. That we are always human and always had
this power. But that we never recognized that, for we were deluged,
bombarded, mesmerized by the trinkets of the ruling class. And this
means all of us: Black, Mexican, White, Indian, Oriental, Gypsy,
all who are members of the working class, of the non-working
class (that is, those who don't have jobs), all who are oppressed.

This means all of us have this power. But the power
only belongs to all of us, not just some or one, but all. And
that was the trick. That was the thing we never understood.
And that is what statement these songs make.

Elaine Brown, from the
Seize the Time album cover (1969)

Songs by Elaine Brown

Jonathan

Jonathan
You weren't there.
You didn't see
Jonathan.
Or do you care,
What do you mean?
Jonathan
He was so young
Picked up a gun
Jonathan.
But a man
Was he.

He'd often go.
He'd hurt her so,
Jonathan.
His mother's eyes
Gleamed mother's
Prize
Jonathan.
What he would do
None of us knew
Jonathan
For a man
Was he.

Some Brothers three,
They had no key.
Jonathan
Saw them in jail.
They had no bail.
Jonathan
The USA
Will have to pay
Jonathan
For the man
Was he.

For they would die
Lest he should try
Jonathan
Oh by his deeds
Give them the keys,
Jonathan.
For those who rule
They couldn't fool
Jonathan
For a man
Was he.

There's more you see
That must be free.
Jonathan
Showed us the way.
What price to pay,
Jonathan.
Open the door,
Just do it for
Jonathan.
You're a man
Like he.

But, you weren't there.
You didn't see
Jonathan.
Or do you care,
What do you mean?
Jonathan,
He was so young
Picked up a gun
Jonathan.
But a man
Was he.

ASSASSINATION

You know I heard the people say
What will you give in your way
I saw them turn, stop
And listen to the people cry
And say, just a life
Is all I got.

In a parade
Of centuries
People cried out,
And said please, please
We want freedom,
Liberation
And just some help in this
Civilization.

You know I heard the people say
What will you give in your way
I saw them turn, stop
And listen to the people cry
And say, just a life
Is all I got.

What did they do.
What did they say.
To justify
Speaking this way
They just fought
And often cried
And then they turned around
Were shot down
And died.

You know I heard the people say
What will you give in your way
I saw them turn, stop
And listen to the people cry
And say, just a life
Is all I got.

Bunchy and John
Walked through this maze
They touched a million lives
In a thousand ways.
Three-score and ten
Never knew them
Twenty-six and twenty-three
Is all they were
Oh can't you see.

And didn't you hear the people say
What will you give in your way
I saw them turn, stop
And listen to the people cry
And say, just a life
Is all I got.

Until We're Free

Yes, I remember
The Yesterdays
The poverty
That you and me
Survived.
For we tried living
On streets that weren't giving
And laughed and cried,
In youth we died
And didn't know.

REFRAIN

Oh yes, my friends
Our history
The memory
Shall carry me
Until we're free
The times we saw
We didn't deserve
Hostility
We couldn't see
It was absurd
But we gave joy,
Each girl and boy
So innocent
Our future bent
Against the wind.

REPEAT REFRAIN

Desperate kisses
In alleyways,
The futile days
They laid to waste
Our little lives . . .
The concrete park,
A stab in the dark
To wrest our soul.
And we were old
Before we grew.

REPEAT REFRAIN

Some friends forgotten,
And some are gone.
How dare they touch
Our little spot
With what they've done.
I miss them all,
But, the future calls
Demanding we
Set ourselves free—
As we should be.

REPEAT REFRAIN

THE BLACK PANTHER PARTY

SEIZE THE TIME

You tell me that the sun belongs
To you and should surround you.
But, when I turn to look
I see they've snatched
The sun from all around you.
Why you hardly seem
To want what's yours
You hardly seem to care.
If you love the sun,
It's where you've come from
Then you had better dare
To Seize The Time
The time is now
Oh, Seize The Time
And you know how.

You tell me that the soul is real
And your soul must survive.
Yet, I see they've taken liberties
With your souls and your lives.
Don't tell me that you lack concern
For all that you must be,
'Cause I know you know you must
    not be turned
And I know that you can see
To Seize The Time
The time is now
Oh, Seize The Time
And you know how.

You worry about liberty
Because you've been denied.
Well, I think that you're mistaken
Or then, you must have lied.
'Cause you do not act like
    those who care
You've never even fought
For the liberty you claim to lack
Or have you never thought
To Seize The Time
The time is now
Oh, Seize The Time
And you know how.

ALL THE YOUNG AND FINE MEN

Oh I was so in love
Last year
Or rather,
The year before.
And if it wasn't death
That claimed them,
It was the hard, cold prison door.

REFRAIN

All such young and fine men
All such well-defined men
And if we remain
Reminded of them,
Then no wall or grave
Can confine them.
I was in love with
Many soldiers
For they were
A part of me
A part of all
I'd grown with
Though they'd somehow grown free.

REPEAT REFRAIN

They came and went
I nodded
A glimpse
Of what could be
A blow for
The downtrodden
Yearning to be free.

REPEAT REFRAIN

As I remember, it's so
Very lonely
When you remember
You can't feel or touch
When remember the touch
Of your brother
You ask, how could they
          do so much . . .

REPEAT REFRAIN

WE SHALL MEET AGAIN

There is a man
Who stands
In all our way
And his greedy hands
Reach out across the world.
But, if we slay this man
We'll have peace in this land
And this glorious struggle
Will be done.

REFRAIN

And, We Shall Meet Again
If we do not die
For that is the price
That might be paid.
But if we pass this way
We shall meet some day
We Shall Meet Again
Yes, if we do not die.

And, what we want
Is just
To have what we need,
And to live
In peace with dignity.
But these few old men
Will not break or bend
So, it's only through their deaths
That we'll be free.

REPEAT REFRAIN

And if we dare
To fight
For what we want,
Sparing none
Who're standing in our way.
The fight is hard and long
But we can't go wrong
For our liberation
Will be won.

REPEAT REFRAIN

VERY BLACK MAN
Just look at a man
If you ever can.
Simply see his face.
See his very Black face.
With no trace of disgrace
With more than a hint
Of pride.

And he feels like a man
Like a very good man
As he places his hand
In mine.
Yes, a very Black hand
That he held in my own
As he led me back home
To my own.

And I'd cry with the man
And I'd die with the man
I'd lie with the man,
'Cause I know that I am
The woman I am
Just with a Very Black Man.

No Time

I want to hold some child
Forever.
Hide his eyes from it all.
Yes, hold some Black child
And rock him
But outside
It's raging
And there is no time
To hold.

I wish to tell some mother,
Dearly,
Tell her all the world is hers,
Tell some dear Black mother
Of her beauty,
But outside
It's burning
And there is no time
To tell.

Yes, I too am weary
With all the pain of it
I wish to love them all
Keep them from
The strain of it all.

Yes, I would hold some man
And kiss him
Live with him until I die
Some wonderful Black man,
I'll miss him . . .
'Cause outside
They're shooting
And there is no time
To try.

BRIDGE

END OF SILENCE

Have you ever stood
In the darkness of night
Screaming silently
You're a man.
Have you ever hoped that
A time would come
When your voice could be heard
In a noon-day sun.
Have you waited so long
'Til your unheard song
Has stripped away your very soul.

REFRAIN

Well then, believe it my friend
That this silence will end
We'll just have to get guns
And be men.
Has a cry to live
When your brain is dead
Made your body tremble so.
And have unseen chains
Of too many years
Hurt you so bad 'til you can't
Shed tears.
Have so many vows
From so many mouths
Made you know that words
Are just words.

REPEAT REFRAIN

You know that dignity
Not just equality
Is what makes a man a man.
And so you laugh at laws
Passed by a silly lot
That tell you to give thanks
For what you've already
Got.
And you can't go on
With this time-worn song
That just won't change the way
You feel.

REPEAT REFRAIN

You don't want to think
You just want to drink
Both the sweet wine and the gall.
You been burning inside
For so long a while
'Til your old-time grin
Is now a crazed-man's smile
And the goal's so clear
And the time so near.
You'll make it or
You'll break the plow.

REPEAT REFRAIN

Yes, it's time you know
Who you really are
And not try whitewash the truth.
You're a man you see
And a man must be
Whatever he'll be or he
Won't be free.
If he's bound up tight
He'll hold back the night
And there won't be no light
For day.

REPEAT REFRAIN

Poetry by Ericka Huggins

We Celebrate All the Fallen Heroes
October 1973

We celebrate all the fallen heroes
across the land
raise flags and monuments to mourn the unknown dead
we give thanks to god on Christmas
we sing hallelujahs to the crucified
jesus on Easter
We empty our pockets in the churches
     where gossip and flashy clothes
        have become holy.
When will we celebrate the lives of
Those who can give us most
     peace,
     security,
love.
When will we praise so many bright
Black and Brown smiling faces
When will we get on our knees to
reality; give what is due to our real
Salvation . . . the babies.
They are our hope
         strength
Their spirit has immortality
They are our future
        Our Children.

Ericka Huggins, deputy
minister of education.
Photographer unknown.

AND THEY KEPT THEM THERE HUNGRY
15 OCTOBER 1973

. . . and they kept them there hungry/poor
and wanted them to learn
were angry when they did not
they beat them
spanked them ('til their full grown hands turned red.)
shouted at them
degraded them,
laughed at them, they
called them "little niggers"
        "wetbacks"
        "half-breeds"

told them they could not learn . . .
       "—take up a trade";
       "—learn to cook";
       "—be a singer" . . . Never
a doctor
a lawyer
never—
a man or
   woman
     We fought that
Now we laugh at the ignorance
     scorned those feelings of fear
    which thwarted thriving minds/
       smiling faces.
We will help our children—
    give them this world
       the moon
       the sun
       the stars
       the universe
       if we can . . .
We will show them how to think
           to be
and they will create a world
          freer
          purer
Not only because we fought, but
because it is on them / we have done enough,
it is their time in history.

STRENGTH
MARCH 1972

Strength is in the oak tree,
Strength too is in the bamboo

The oak bends not with the wind
The bamboo sways / not breaks
$\qquad\qquad\qquad$ but bends ...

to know the people
be like the bamboo
bend with the winds of change

Fire & Rain
1 May 1972

as intense as a flame—
    warning us
    comforting us;
blinding
burning those who can not bear to feel
                       see it.
as thorough and far-reaching as a
summer rain
      refreshing us
    washing away fears/selfish things;
drowning
choking those who can not be cleansed by the truth,
who can not hold out their hands and receive drops of the
      clear water of freedom
like fire and rain
is our love for the people

LET THE FAULT BE WITH THE MAN
AUGUST 1972

let the fault be with the man
whose desires overwhelm his humanness
let the fault be with the woman
who places emphasis on comfort of the body
rather than on the stability of the mind
let the fault be with those who judge one's character
by one's ability to be 'polite'
let the fault be with those who fear the nature of
development
rather than those whose development is natural,
open, real.
there is neither a difference
or an intrusion
that alters our views of people
It is the futile quest for the perfect in ourselves,
the morally correct.
if we are revolutionaries, then what is correct
must be that which provides for our survival.
if we should survive
then let it be for real reasons/not for reasons derived
from fear.
we can only for so long as we live
remain the people that we are—fighting,
struggling, dying,
in the long run it will be those whose
character is steadfast who will help us win.
let the fault be then with the man or woman
whose personal views create our failure.

I Remember Times

1971

i remember times when i had love
to give and there was no one to love
i remember times when i had truths
to exchange and everyone regretted it
i remember when i found that life
is struggle and they told me that
i wished it that way
i remember times when i cried
while everyone laughed hysterically
i remember and now while i am
calm everyone is screaming
       yelling.
       pleading with me
to tell them when/how/where/what we
found out and i just remember
times . . .

Emory Douglas
Art for the People's Sake

O n October 2, 1972, Emory Douglas, the popular People's Artist for the Black
Panther Party whose works regularly adorn the back page of The Black
Panther *newspaper, spoke at Fisk University in Nashville, Tennessee. In
speaking to the assembly of predominantly Black students and professors,
Emory explained, in relationship to a Black artist's responsibilities, how art
could be used as a vehicle to elevate the consciousness of Black and poor communities: "No artist can sit in an ivory tower. . . . The artist has to be down on
the ground; he has to hear the sounds of the people, the cries of the people, the
suffering of the people, the laughter of the people—the dark side and the bright
side of our lives."*

The text of that Nashville speech follows.

*Emory Douglas's works have been exhibited throughout the United States,
Africa, Asia, and Latin America and have been reproduced widely by third world
publications as well as filmed for television both within this country and abroad.
In addition, Emory is a university lecturer on "Art in Service for the People" and
is the art instructor at the Community Learning Center.*

All Power to the People.

I'm very happy to be here as a representative from the Black Panther Party.
Tonight, I would like to discuss with you the relationship of the Black artist to
the Black community. We must take that as a very serious thing, because when
we look at the world today, we see that we have very serious problems.

We have to understand that we have been duped into believing that we are supposed to criticize all the Greek, the Roman, and all the ancient European art. We have been taught how to criticize them; we have been told how to criticize them. But what happens when we criticize them? We begin to try to duplicate them. We begin to spend our time in trying to copy something that is old, that is decadent, that is out of date . . . like the work of Leonardo da Vinci and those other painters.

But we have a greater enemy in relationship to art. We have a greater enemy, I would say, in commercial art. What is commercial art? It is a method of persuasion, mind control; it oppresses Black people. If we look around our community, what do we see? We see billboards, with advertising, that tell us what to buy, how to buy. And we go out and buy—our own oppression.

It [advertising] tells us to go out and buy a house, for 6 percent interest; we buy the house and suffer for the next twenty years trying to pay for that house. What am I trying to tell you? It's this: we have to take that structure of commercial art and add a brand-new content to it, a content that will serve the interests of Black people. We see that they [the capitalists] have done what we should be doing. They have analyzed how to appeal to Black people, so that Black people will go out and buy. They have begun to analyze how to relate to Black people so that we will continue to suffer—peacefully.

But we say that if we take this structure of commercial art and add a brand-new content to it, then we will have begun to analyze Black people and our situation for the purpose of raising our consciousness to the oppression that we are subjected to. We would use commercial art for the purpose of educating Black people, not oppressing them. So I made that statement in the beginning so that perhaps I could get off into an outline with a few questions in regards to who art is for. I would say that art is for the masses of Black people; we must bombard the masses with art. We cannot do this in an art gallery, because our people do not go to art galleries; we can't afford to go to art galleries . . .

We have to put our art all over the United States, wherever Black people are. If we're talking about an art that serves our people, if we're truly talking about an art that is in the interests of Black people, then we have to use, again, the structure of commercial art.

Isn't it true, that wherever you look, all over the country, you see billboards selling a product? Isn't it true, that whenever you look in a magazine, it's selling a product? Why can't we use that same structure in relationship to ourselves, to raise the consciousness of Black people; in regards to using our art in that same form; putting it into posters, thousands upon thousands of posters, so that they can be distributed, so all Black people across the country can get the message . . .

We also have the question of how to define art (for ourselves). Many would say that we define art from a dictionary, but we know that the problems are too complicated, too complex, to define art from a dictionary. We cannot even define art by a board of directors. We say that art is defined by the people, because the people are the ones who make art.

If we are truly drawing the people, if we are trying to reflect the society which we live in, then that means that we, the artists, will draw the people; but the people are the real artists. No artist can sit in an ivory tower, discussing the problems of the day, and come up with a solution on a piece of paper. The artist has to be down on the ground; he has to hear the sounds of the people, the cries of the people, the suffering of the people, the laughter of the people—the dark side and the bright side of our lives.

The dark side is the oppression, the suffering, the decadent living, which we always expose. But the bright side is that which we praise: beautiful Black people who are rising up and resisting. There is a difference between exposing and praising. We don't expose the people; we expose the system (of the United States) in relationship to art, but we praise the people in relationship to art. We show them as the heroes; we put them on the stage. We make characters of our people (around the idea of what they know life should be about).

We can talk about politics in art, and many people will get confused on the issue in regard to what is primary. Is it the political situation, or the artistic situation? Art is subordinate to politics. The political situation is greater than the artistic situation. A picture can express a thousand words, but action is supreme. Politics is based on action; politics starts with a hungry stomach, with dilapidated housing. Politics does not start in the political arena; it starts right down there in the community, where the suffering is. If art is subordinate, then, to the political situation, wouldn't it be true that the artist must begin to interpret the hungry stomach, bad housing, all of these things and transform these things into something that would raise the consciousness of Black people? I think that would be the most logical thing to do.

In regard to criticism in art: we praise all that which helps us in our resistance for future liberation. We condemn all those things in art that are opposed to our liberation.

If we, as artists, do not understand our role and relationship to the society, to the political situation and the survival of Black people, then how can we create art that will project survival? How can we begin to create an art that shows a love—a true love—for Black people? When the artist begins to love the people, to appreciate them, he or she will begin to draw the people differently; we can begin to interpret and project into our art something that is much greater than it was before. Freedom, justice, liberation: all those things that we could not apply to our art before.

How do we judge art . . . By the subjective intentions of the person (the motive)? Or do we judge art by the effect it has? We have to take both of these things into consideration. The motive is the idea; the idea that I believe a drawing should be drawn in a particular manner is only my personal thought. So, what I have to do is take into consideration if the art is going to correspond to what's happening in the community; if it is going to elevate the level of consciousness of Black people in the community. That means that I have to go out into the community and investigate in order to find out if what I want to draw is going to correspond with the reality of the community. Then I will be taking into consideration not only my motive, which is my own personal feeling, but I would also be taking into consideration the effect: the actual, practical everyday activity that goes on in the community. We have to link up the two . . .

You see, another thing that the reactionary system does is to carry on a pacification program by using art. They tell us that we should not draw things that deal with liberation, that we should not draw things that deal with violence. But at the same time they perpetrate the worst violence on the planet Earth while they have us drawing pictures of flowers and butterflies. We must understand that when there are over twenty million people in this country, hungry, then we, as artists, have something we must deal with . . .

PART IV
Book Excerpts

Introduction to Book Excerpts

The theoretical writings of the Black Panther Party serve as a record of the party's history, its developing ideology, and its analysis of the correct handling of the revolutionary struggle—both here in the United States and throughout the third world. Any political organization that is seriously acting as the vanguard of the people, which the Black Panther Party is doing in America, must state its analysis on important issues so that the people will understand these issues, which directly relate to their oppression. Once they have a full understanding of the issues, they will be able to move to end that oppression.

Revolutionary Suicide, the autobiography of Huey P. Newton, leader and chief theoretician of the Black Panther Party, is a personal account of Black oppression and resistance in America. In the following excerpts from the book, Brother Huey defines the concepts behind the Black Panther Party's programs and organizing activities.

Other books by Huey P. Newton include *To Die for the People*, a collection of essays on the Black Panther Party and the Black liberation struggle, and *In Search of Common Ground*, coauthored by the world-famous psychoanalyst Erik H. Erikson. The latter book is a record of the two men's 1971 conversations, first at Yale University in New Haven, Connecticut, and later that same year in Oakland, California.

The genius of Brother George Jackson, assassinated field marshal of the Black Panther Party, is shown in the excerpt from *Blood in My Eye*, his last major work completed before his death. Not only did Brother George serve as an expert revolutionary theorist, but he put that theory into practice as America's foremost prison organizer.

In a departure from the party's theoretical writings, this section also includes excerpts from *And Bid Him Sing*, a novel written by Brother David G. DuBois, talented veteran journalist and editor-in-chief of The Black Panther Intercommunal News Service. This suspenseful book revolves around the experiences of a Black American living in Egypt at the time of the outbreak of the 1967 Middle East war.

Revolutionary Suicide

by Huey P. Newton

*T*he concept of revolutionary suicide, developed by Huey P. Newton and outlined in the first selection that follows, is one of the Black Panther Party's
major philosophical beliefs. At the heart of this concept is the view that it is
better to oppose those reactionary forces that would drive one to self-murder than
to endure them and be destroyed by them in the end. "Freedom," the second selection presented, deals with the prison experiences of the leader and chief theoretician of the Black Panther Party. Huey, in this selection, writes, "Jail is an odd
place to find freedom, but that was the place I found mine." Both selections are
taken from Huey P. Newton's autobiographical work, Revolutionary Suicide.

Revolutionary Suicide: The Way of Liberation

For twenty-two months in the California Men's Colony at San Luis Obispo,
after my first trial for the death of Patrolman John Frey, I was almost continually in solitary confinement. There, in a four-by-six cell, except for books and
papers relating to my case, I was allowed no reading material. Despite the rigid
enforcement of this rule, inmates sometimes slipped magazines under my door
when the guards were not looking. One that reached me was the May 1970 issue
of *Ebony* magazine. It contained an article written by Lacy Banko summariz-
ing the work of Dr. Herbert Hendin, who had done a comparative study on suicide among Black people in the major American cities. Dr. Hendin found that
the suicide rate among Black men between the ages of nineteen and thirty-five
had doubled in the past ten to fifteen years, surpassing the rate for whites in

the same age range. The article had—and still has—a profound effect on me. I have thought long and hard about its implications.

The *Ebony* article brought to mind Durkheim's classic study, *Suicide*, a book I had read earlier while studying sociology at Oakland City College. To Durkheim all types of suicide are related to social conditions. He maintains that the primary cause of suicide is not individual temperament but forces in the social environment. In other words, suicide is caused primarily by external factors, not internal ones. As I thought about the conditions of Black people and about Dr. Hendin's study, I began to develop Durkheim's analysis and apply it to the Black experience in the United States. This eventually led to the concept of "revolutionary suicide."

To understand revolutionary suicide it is first necessary to have an idea of reactionary suicide, for the two are very different. Dr. Hendin was describing reactionary suicide: the reaction of a man who takes his own life in response to social conditions that overwhelm him and condemn him to helplessness. The young Black men in his study had been deprived of human dignity, crushed by oppressive forces, and denied their right to live as proud and free human beings.

A section of Dostoevsky's *Crime and Punishment* provides a good analogy. One of the characters, Marmeladov, a very poor man, argues that poverty is not a vice. In poverty, he says, a man can attain the innate nobility of soul that is not possible in beggary; for while society may drive the poor man out with a stick, the beggar will be swept out with a broom. Why? Because the beggar is totally demeaned, his dignity lost. Finally, bereft of self-respect, immobilized by fear and despair, he sinks into self-murder. This is reactionary suicide.

SPIRITUAL DEATH

Connected to reactionary suicide, although even more painful and degrading, is a spiritual death that has been the experience of millions of Black people in the United States. This death is found everywhere today in the Black community. Its victims have ceased to fight the forms of oppression that drink their blood. The common attitude has long been: What's the use? If a man rises up against a power as great as the United States, he will not survive. Believing this, many Blacks have been driven to a death of the spirit rather than of the flesh, lapsing into lives of quiet desperation. Yet all the while, in the heart of every Black, there is the hope that life will somehow change in the future.

I do not think that life will change for the better without an assault on the Establishment, which goes on exploiting the wretched of the earth. This belief lies at the heart of the concept of revolutionary suicide. Thus it is better to oppose the forces that would drive me to self-murder than to endure them. Although I risk the likelihood of death, there is at least the possibility, if not the probability, of changing intolerable conditions. This possibility is important, because much in human existence is based upon hope without any real understanding of the odds. Indeed, we are all—Black and white alike—ill in the same way, mortally ill. But before we die, how shall we live? I say with hope and dignity, and if premature death is the result, that death has a meaning reactionary suicide can never have; it is the price of self-respect.

Revolutionary suicide does not mean that I and my comrades have a death wish; it means just the opposite. We have such a strong desire to live with hope and human dignity that existence without them is impossible. When reactionary forces crush us, we must move against these forces, even at the risk of death. We will have to be driven out with a stick.

Che Guevara said that to a revolutionary death is the reality and victory the dream. Because the revolutionary lives so dangerously, his survival is a miracle. Bakunin, who spoke for the most militant wing of the First International, made a similar statement in his *Revolutionary Catechism*. To him, the first lesson a revolutionary must learn is that he is a doomed man. Unless he understands this, he does not grasp the essential meaning of his life.

SERIOUSNESS

When Fidel Castro and his small band were in Mexico preparing for the Cuban Revolution, many of the comrades had little understanding of Bakunin's rule. A few hours before they set sail, Fidel went from man to man asking who should be notified in case of death. Only then did the deadly seriousness of the revolution hit home. Their struggle was no longer romantic. The scene had been exciting and animated, but when the simple, overwhelming question of death arose, everyone fell silent.

Many so-called revolutionaries in this country, Black and white, are not prepared to accept this reality. The Black Panthers are not suicidal; neither do we romanticize the consequences of revolution in our lifetime. Other so-called revolutionaries cling to an illusion that they might have their revolution and die of old age. That cannot be.

I do not expect to live through our revolution, and most serious comrades probably share my realism. Therefore, the expression "revolution in our lifetime" means something different to me than it does to other people who use it. I think the revolution will grow in my lifetime, but I do not expect to enjoy its fruits. That would be a contradiction. The reality will be grimmer.

I have no doubt that the revolution will triumph. The people of the world will prevail, seize power, seize the means of production, and wipe out racism, capitalism, reactionary intercommunalism—reactionary suicide. The people will win a new world. Yet when I think of individuals in the revolution, I cannot predict their survival. Revolutionaries must accept this fact, especially the Black revolutionaries in America, whose lives are in constant danger from the evils of a colonial society. Considering how we must live, it is not hard to accept the concept of revolutionary suicide. In this we are different from white radicals. They are not faced with genocide.

The greater, more immediate problem is the survival of the entire world. If the world does not change, all its people will be threatened by the greed, exploitation, and violence of the power structure in the American empire. The handwriting is on the wall. The United States is jeopardizing its own existence and the existence of all humanity. If Americans knew the disasters that lay ahead, they would transform this society tomorrow for their own preservation. The Black Panther Party is in the vanguard of the revolution that seeks to relieve this country of its crushing burden of guilt. We are determined to establish true equality and the means for creative work.

Some see our struggle as a symbol of the trend toward suicide among Blacks. Scholars and academics in particular have been quick to make this accusation. They fail to perceive differences. Jumping off a bridge is not the same as moving to wipe out the overwhelming force of an oppressive army. When scholars call our actions suicidal, they should be logically consistent and describe all historical revolutionary movements in the same way. Thus the American colonists, the French of the late eighteenth century, the Russians of 1917, the Jews of Warsaw, the Cubans, the NLF, the North Vietnamese—any people who struggle against a brutal and powerful force—are suicidal. Also, if the Black Panthers symbolize the suicidal trend among Blacks, then the whole third world is suicidal, because the third world fully intends to resist and overcome the ruling class of the United States. If scholars wish to carry their analysis further, they must come to terms with that four-fifths of the world that is bent on wiping out the power of the empire. In those terms the third world would be transformed from suicidal to homicidal, although homicide is the unlawful taking of life, and the third world is involved only in defense. Is the coin then turned? Is the government of the United States suicidal? I think so.

REDEFINITION

With this redefinition, the term "revolutionary suicide" is not as simplistic as it might seem initially. In coining the phrase, I took two knowns and combined them to make an unknown, a neoteric phrase in which the word "revolutionary" transforms the word "suicide" into an idea that has different dimensions and meanings applicable to a new and complex situation.

My prison experience is a good example of revolutionary suicide in action, for prison is a microcosm of the outside world. From the beginning of my sentence I defied the authorities by refusing to cooperate; as a result, I was confined to "lockup," a solitary cell. As the months passed and I remained steadfast, they came to regard my behavior as suicidal. I was told that I would crack and break under the strain. I did not break, nor did I retreat from my position. I grew strong.

If I had submitted to their exploitation, done their will, it would have killed my spirit and condemned me to a living death. To cooperate in prison meant reactionary suicide to me. While solitary confinement can be physically and mentally destructive, my actions were taken with an understanding of the risk. I had to suffer through a certain situation; by doing so, my resistance told them that I rejected all they stood for. Even though my struggle might have harmed my health, even killed me, I looked upon it as a way of raising the consciousness of the other inmates as a contribution to the ongoing revolution. Only resistance can destroy the pressures that cause reactionary suicide.

The concept of revolutionary suicide is not defeatist or fatalistic. On the contrary, it conveys an awareness of reality in combination with the possibility of hope—reality because the revolutionary must always be prepared to face death, and hope because it symbolized a resolute determination to bring about change. Above all, it demands that the revolutionary see his death and his life as one piece. Chairman Mao says that death comes to all of us, but it varies in its significance: to die for the reactionary is lighter than a feather; to die for the revolution is heavier than Mount Tai.

FREEDOM

Jail is an odd place to find freedom, but that was the place I first found mine: in the Alameda County Jail in Oakland in 1964. This jail is located on the tenth floor of the Alameda County Courthouse, the huge, white building we call "Moby Dick." When I was falsely convicted of the assault against Odell Lee, Judge Dieden sent me there to await sentencing. Shortly after I arrived, I was made a trusty, which gave me an opportunity to move about freely. Conditions were not good; in fact, the place blew up a few weeks later, when the inmates refused to go on eating starches and split-pea soup at almost every meal, and went on a food strike. I joined them. When we were brought our split-pea soup, we hurled it back through the bars, all over the walls, and refused to lock up in our cells.

I was the only trusty who took part in the strike, and because I could move between cell blocks, they charged me with organizing it. True, I had carried a few messages back and forth, but I was not an organizer then. Not that it mattered to the jail administration. Trusties were supposed to go along with the Establishment in everything, and since I could not do that, I was slapped with the organizing label and put in the "hole"—what Black prisoners call the "soul breaker."

I was twenty-two years old, and I had been in jail before on various beefs, mostly burglary and petty larceny. My parents were pretty sick of me in my late teens and the years following, so I had to depend on Sonny Man to come up from Los Angeles, or wherever he was, to bail me out. Since I had been "given" to him, he came whenever he could. But sometimes I could not find him. At any rate, I was no stranger to jail by 1964, although I had never been in extreme solitary confinement.

Within jail, there are four levels of confinement: the main line, segregation, isolation, and solitary—the "soul breaker." You can be in jail in jail, but the soul breaker is your "last" end of the world. In 1964, there were two of these deprivation cells at the Alameda County Courthouse; each was four and a half feet wide, by six feet long, by ten feet high. The floor was dark red rubber tile, and the walls were black. If the guards wanted to, they could turn on a light in the ceiling, but I was always kept in the dark, and nude. That is part of the deprivation, why the soul breaker is called a strip cell. Sometimes the prisoner in the other cell would get a blanket, but they never gave me one. He sometimes got toilet paper, too—the limit was two squares—and when he begged for more, he was told no, that is part of the punishment. There was no bunk, no washbasin, no toilet, nothing but bare floors, bare walls, a solid steel door, and a round hole four inches in diameter and six inches deep in the middle of the floor. The prisoner was supposed to urinate and defecate in this hole.

A half-gallon milk carton filled with water was my liquid for the week.

Twice a day and always at night the guards brought a little cup of cold split-pea soup, right out of the can. Sometimes during the day they brought "fruit loaf," a patty of cooked vegetables mashed together into a little ball. When I first went in there, I wanted to eat and stay healthy, but soon I realized that was another trick, because when I ate I had to defecate. At night no light came in under the door. I could not even find the hole if I wanted to. If I was desperate, I had to search with my hand; when I found it, the hole was always slimy with the filth that had gone in before. I was just like a mole looking for the sun; I hated finding it when I did. After a few days the hole filled up and overflowed, so that I could not lie down without wallowing in my own waste. Once every week or two the guards ran a hose into the cell and washed out the urine and defecation. This cleared the air for a while and made it all right to take a deep breath. I had been told I would break before the fifteen days were up. Most men did. After two or three days they would begin to scream and beg for someone to come and take them out, and the captain would pay a visit and say, "We don't want to treat you this way. Just come out now and abide by the rules and don't be so arrogant. We'll treat you fairly. The doors here are large." To tell the truth, after two or three days I was in bad shape. Why I did not break I do not know. Stubbornness, probably. I did not want to beg. Certainly my resistance was not connected to any kind of ideology or program. That came later. Anyway, I did not scream and beg; I learned the secrets of survival.

One secret was the same that Mahatma Gandhi learned—to take little sips of nourishment, just enough to keep up one's strength, but never enough to have to defecate until the fifteen days were up. That way I kept the air somewhat clean and did not have the overflow. I did the same with water, taking little sips every few hours. My body absorbed all of it, and I did not have to urinate.

There was another, more important secret, one that took longer to learn. During the day a little light showed in the two-inch crack at the bottom of the steel door. At night, as the sun went down and the lights clicked off one by one, I heard all the cells closing and all the locks. I held my hands up in front of my face, and soon I could not see them. For me, that was the testing time, the time when I had to save myself or break.

Outside jail, the brain is always being bombarded by external stimuli. These ordinary sights and sounds of life help to keep our mental processes in order, rational. In deprivation, you have to somehow replace the stimuli, provide an interior environment for yourself. Ever since I was a little boy I have been able to overcome stress by calling up pleasant thoughts. So very soon I began to reflect on the most soothing parts of my past, not to keep out any evil thoughts, but to reinforce myself in some kind of rewarding experience. Here I learned something. This was different.

When I had a pleasant memory, what was I to do with it? Should I throw it out and get another or try to keep it to entertain myself as long as possible? If you are not disciplined, a strange thing happens. The pleasant thought comes, and then another and another, like quick cuts flashing vividly across a movie screen. At first they are organized. Then they start to pick up speed, pushing in on top of one another, going faster, faster, faster, faster. The pleasant thoughts are not so pleasant now; they are horrible and grotesque caricatures whirling around in your head. Stop! I heard myself say, stop, stop, stop. I did not scream. I was able to stop them. Now what do I do?

I started to exercise, especially when I heard the jangle of keys as the guards came with the split-pea soup and fruit loaf. I would not scream; I would not apologize, even though they came every day, saying they would let me out if I gave in. When they were coming, I would get up and start my calisthenics, and when they went away, I would start the pleasant thoughts again. If I was too tired to stand, I would lie down and find myself on my back. Later, I learned that my position, with my back arched and only my shoulders and tight buttocks touching the floor, was a Zen Buddhist posture. I did not know it then, of course; I just found myself on my back. When the thoughts started coming again to entertain me and when the same thing happened with the speed-up, faster, faster, I would say, stop! and start again.

Over a span of time—I do not know how long it took—I mastered my thoughts. I could start them and stop them; I could slow them down and speed them up. It was a very conscious exercise. For a while, I feared I would lose control. I could not think; I could not stop thinking. Only later did I learn through practice to go at the speed I wanted. I call them film clips, but they are really thought patterns, the most vivid pictures of my family, girls, good tunes. Soon I could lie with my back arched for hours on end, and I placed no importance on the passage of time. Control. I learned to control my food, my body, and my mind through a deliberate act of will.

After fifteen days the guards pulled me out and sent me back to a regular cell for twenty-four hours, where I took a shower and saw a medical doctor and a psychiatrist. They were worried that prisoners would become mentally disorganized in such deprivation. Then, because I had not repented, they sent me back to the hole. By then it held no fears for me. I had won my freedom.

Soul breakers exist because the authorities know that such conditions would drive them to the breaking point, but when I resolved that they would not conquer my will, I became stronger than they were. I understood them better than they understood me. No longer dependent on the things of the world, I felt really free for the first time in my life. In the past I had been like my jailers; I had pursued the goals of capitalistic America. Now I had a higher freedom.

Most people who know me do not realize that I have been in and out of jail for the past twelve years. They know only of my eleven months in solitary in 1967, waiting for the murder trial to begin, and the twenty-two months at the Penal Colony after that. But 1967 would not have been possible without 1964. I could not have handled the Penal Colony solitary without the soul breaker behind me. Therefore, I cannot tell inexperienced young comrades to go into jail and into solitary, that that is the way to defy the authorities and exercise their freedom. I know what solitary can do to a man.

The strip cell has been outlawed throughout the United States. Prisoners I talk to in California tell me it is no longer in use on the West Coast. That was the work of Charles Garry, the lawyer who defended me in 1968, when he fought the case of Warren Wells, a Black Panther accused of shooting a policeman. The Superior Court of California said it was an outrage to human decency to put any man through such extreme deprivation. Of course, prisons have their ways, and out there right now, somewhere, prisoners without lawyers are probably lying in their own filth in the soul breaker.

I was in the hole for a month. My sentence, when it came, was for six months on the county farm at Santa Rita, about fifty miles south of Oakland. This is an honor camp with no walls, and the inmates are not locked up. There is a barbed-wire fence, but anyone can easily walk off during the daytime. The inmates work at tending livestock, harvesting crops, and doing other farm work.

I was not in the honor camp long. A few days after I arrived, I had a fight with a fat Black inmate named Bojack, who served in the mess hall. Bojack was a diligent enforcer of small helpings, and I was a "dipper." Whenever Bojack turned away, I would dip for more with my spoon. One day he tried to prevent me from dipping, and I called him for protecting the oppressor's interests and smashed him with a steel tray. When they pulled me off him, I was hustled next door to Graystone, the maximum security prison at Santa Rita.

Here, prisoners are locked up all day inside a stone building. Not only that. I was put in solitary confinement for the remaining months of my sentence. Because of my experience in the hole, I could survive. Still, I did not submit willingly. The food was as bad in Graystone as it had been in Alameda, and I constantly protested about that and the lack of heat in my cell. Half the time we had no heat at all.

Wherever you go in prison there are disturbed inmates. One on my block at Santa Rita screamed night and day as loudly as he could; his vocal cords seemed made of iron. From time to time, the guards came into his cell and threw buckets of cold water on him. Gradually, as the inmate wore down, the scream became a croak and then a squeak and then a whisper. Long after he gave out, the sound lingered in my head.

The Santa Rita administration finally got disgusted with my continual complaints and protests and shipped me back to the jail in Oakland, where I spent the rest of my time in solitary. By then I was used to the cold. Even now, I do not like any heat at all wherever I stay, no matter what the outside temperature. Even so, the way I was treated told me a lot about those who devised such punishment. I know them well.

Toward the United Front
from *Blood in My Eye* by George Jackson

*T*he following essay, "Toward the United Front," was taken from Blood in My Eye, *the last work written by George Jackson, the late field marshal of the Black Panther Party. Although this one essay provides only a glimpse of the total genius that Comrade George possessed, it very amply shows why George Jackson is still one of the best loved, most respected and widely quoted activist/ authors a full three years following his assassination on August 21, 1971, by San Quentin prison guards. It also shows why millions of people throughout the world continue to reiterate the people's cry: George Jackson lives!*

A new unitarian and progressive current has sprung up in the movement centering on political prisoners. How can this unitarian conduct be developed further in the face of determined resistance from the establishment? How can it be used to isolate reactionary elements?

Unitary conduct implies a "search" for those elements in our present situation that can become the basis for joint action. It involves a conscious reaching for the relevant, the entente, and especially, in our case, the reconcilable.

Throughout the centralizing authoritarian process of Amerikan history, the ruling classes have found it necessary to discourage and punish any genuine opposition to hierarchy. But there have always been individuals and groups who rejected the ideal of two unequal societies, existing one on top of the other.

The men who place themselves above the rest of society through guile, fortuitous outcome of circumstance, and sheer brutality have developed two principal institutions to deal with any and all serious disobedience—the prison and institutionalized racism.

There are more prisons of all categories in the United States than in all other countries of the world combined. At all times there are two-thirds of a million people or more confined to these prisons. Hundreds are destined to be legally executed, thousands more quasi-legally. Other thousands will never again have any freedom of movement barring a revolutionary change in all the institutions that combine to make up the order of things.

One-third of a million people may not seem like a great number compared with the total population of two hundred million. However, compared with the one million who are responsible for all the affairs of men within the extended state, it constitutes a striking contrast. What I want to explore now are a few of the subtle elements that I have observed to be standing in the path of a much-needed united front (nonsectarian) to effectively reverse this legitimized rip-off.

Prisons were not institutionalized on such a massive scale by the people. Most people realize that crime is simply the result of a grossly disproportionate distribution of wealth and privilege, a reflection of the present state of property relations. There are no wealthy men on death row, and so few in the general prison population that we can discount them altogether. Imprisonment is an aspect of class struggle from the outset. It is the creation of a closed society, which attempts to isolate those individuals who disregard the structures of a hypocritical establishment as well as those who attempt to challenge it on a mass basis.

Throughout its history, the United States has used its prisons to suppress any organized efforts to challenge its legitimacy—from its attempts to break up the early Working Men's Benevolent Association to the banning of the Communist Party during what I regard as the fascist takeover of this country, to the attempts to destroy the Black Panther Party.

Hypocrisy

The hypocrisy of Amerikan fascism forces it to conceal its attack on political offenders by the legal fiction of conspiracy laws and highly sophisticated frame-ups. The masses must be taught to understand the true function of prisons. Why do they exist in such numbers? What is the real underlying economic motive of crime and the official definition of types of offenders or victims? The people must learn that when one "offends" the totalitarian state it is patently not an offense against the people of that state, but an assault upon the privilege of the privileged few.

Could anything be more ridiculous than the language of blatantly political indictments: "The People of the State . . . vs. Angela Davis and Ruchell McGee" or "The People of the State . . . vs. Bobby Seale and Ericka Huggins." What people? Clearly the hierarchy, the armed minority.

We must educate the people in the real causes of economic crimes. They must be made to realize that even crimes of passion are the psychosocial effects of an economic order that was decadent a hundred years ago. All crime can be traced to objective socioeconomic conditions—socially productive or counter-productive activity. In all cases, it is determined by the economic system, the method of economic organization. "The People of the State . . . vs. John Doe" is as tenuous as the clearly political frame-ups. It's like stating "The People vs. The People." Man against himself. Official definitions of crime are simply attempts by the establishment to suppress the forces of progress.

Prisoners must be reached and made to understand that they are victims of social injustice. This is my task working from within (while I'm here, my persuasion is that the war goes on no matter where one may find himself on bourgeois-dominated soil). The sheer numbers of the prisoner class and the terms of their existence make them a mighty reservoir of revolutionary potential. Working alone and from within a steel-enclosed society, there is very little that people like myself can do to awaken the restrained potential revolutionary outside the walls. That is part of the task of the "Prison Movement."

The Prison Movement, the August 7th movement, and all similar efforts educate the people in the illegitimacy of establishment power and hint at the ultimate goal of revolutionary consciousness at every level of struggle. The goal is always the same: the creation of an infrastructure capable of fielding a people's army.

Each of us should understand that revolution is aggressive. The manipulators of the system cannot or will not meet our legitimate demands. Eventually this will move us all into a violent encounter with the system. These are the terminal years of capitalism, and as we move into more and more basic challenges to its rule, history clearly forewarns us that when the prestige of power fails a violent episode precedes its transformation.

We can attempt to limit the scope and range of violence in revolution by mobilizing as many partisans as possible at every level of socioeconomic life. But given the hold that the ruling class has on this country, and its history of violence, nothing could be more certain than civil disorders, perhaps even civil war. I don't dread either. There are no good aspects of monopoly capital, so no reservations need be recognized in its destruction. Monopoly capital is the enemy. It crushes the life force of all of the people. It must be completely destroyed, as quickly as possible, utterly, totally, ruthlessly, relentlessly destroyed.

With this as a common major goal, it would seem that antiestablishment forces would find little difficulty in developing common initiatives and methods consistent with the goals of mass society. Regretfully, this has not been the case. Only the prison movement has shown any promise of cutting across the ideological, racial, and cultural barricades that have blocked the natural coalition of left-wing forces at all times in the past.

So this movement must be used to provide an example for the partisans engaged at other levels of struggle. The issues involved and the dialectic that flows from an understanding of the clear objective existence of overt oppression could be the springboard for our entry into the tide of increasing worldwide socialist consciousness.

In order to create a united left, whose aim is the defense of political prisoners and prisoners in general, we must renounce the idea that all participants must be of one mind, and should work at the problem from a single party line or with a single party line or with a single method. The reverse of this is actually desirable. "From all according to ability."

Each partisan, outside the vanguard elements, should work at radicalizing in the area of their natural environment the places where they pursue their normal lives when not attending the rallies and demonstrations. The vanguard elements (organized party workers of all ideological persuasions) should go among the people concentrated at the rallying point with consciousness-raising strategy, promoting commitment and providing concrete, clearly defined activity. The vanguard elements must search out people who can and will contribute to the building of the commune, the infrastructure, with pen and clipboard in hand. For those who aren't ready to take that step, a "packet" of pamphlets should be provided for their education.

Vanguard Party

All of this, of course, means that we are moving, and on a mass level: not all in our separate directions—but firmly under the disciplined and principled leadership of the Vanguard Black Panther Communist Party. "One simply cannot act without a head." Democratic centralism is the only way to deal effectively with the Amerikan ordeal. The central committee of the people's vanguard party must make its presence felt throughout the various levels of the overall movement.

With the example of unity in the prison movement, we can begin to break the old behavioral patterns that have repeatedly allowed bourgeois capitalism, its imperialism and fascism, to triumph over the last several decades. We tap a massive potential reservoir of partisans for cadre work. We make it possible to begin to address one of the most complex psychosocial byproducts that economic man with his private enterprise has manufactured—Racism.

I've saved this most critical barrier to our needs of unity for last. Racism is a matter of ingrained traditional attitudes conditioned through institutions. For some, it is as natural a reflex as breathing. The psychosocial effects of segregated environments compounded by bitter class repression have served in the past to render the progressive movement almost totally impotent.

The major obstacle to a united left in this country is White racism. There are three categories of White racists: the overt, self-satisfied racist who doesn't attempt to hide his antipathy; the self-interdicting racist who harbors and nurtures racism in spite of his best efforts; and the unconscious racist, who has no awareness of his racist preconceptions.

I deny the existence of Black racism outright; by fiat I deny it. Too much Black blood has flowed between the chasm that separates the races. It's fundamentally unfair to expect the Black man to differentiate at a glance between the various kinds of White racists. What the apologists term Black racism is either a healthy defense reflex on the part of the sincere Black partisan who is attempting to deal with the realistic problems of survival and elevation, or the racism of the government stooge organs.

As Black partisans, we must recognize and allow for the existence of all three types of racists. We must understand their presence as an effect of the system. It is the system that must be crushed, for it continues to manufacture new and deeper contradictions of both class and race. Once it is destroyed, we may be able to address the problems of racism at an even more basic level. But we must also combat racism while we are in the process of destroying the system.

The self-interdicting racist, no matter what his acquired conviction or ideology, will seldom be able to contribute with his actions in any really concrete way. His role in revolution, barring a change of basic character, will be minimal throughout. Whether the basic character of a man can be changed at all is still a question. But . . . we have in the immediacy of the "Issues in Question" the perfect opportunity to test the validity of materialist philosophy again, because we don't have to guess. We have the means of proof.

The need for unitarian conduct goes much deeper than the liberation of Angela, Bobby, Ericka, Magee, Los Siete, Tijerina, white draft-resisters, and now the indomitable and faithful James Carr. We have fundamental strategy to be proved—tested and proved. The activity surrounding the protection and liberation of people who fight for us is an important aspect of the struggle. But it is important only if it provides new initiatives that redirect and advance the revolution under new progressive methods.

There must be a collective redirection of the old guard—the factory and union agitator—with the campus activist who can counter the ill effects of fascism at its training site, and with the lumpen proletariat intellectuals who possess revolutionary scientific-socialist attitudes to deal with the masses of street people already living outside the system. They must work toward developing the unity of the pamphlet and the silenced pistol. Black, brown, and white are all victims together.

At the end of this massive collective struggle, we will uncover our new man, the unpredictable culmination of the revolutionary process. He will be better equipped to wage the real struggle, the permanent struggle after the revolution—the one for new relationships between men.

And Bid Him Sing

by David Graham DuBois

A nd Bid Him Sing *is a new novel written by David G. DuBois, editor-in-chief of The Black Panther Intercommunal News Service. The novel revolves around the life of Suliman Ibn Ismael, a Black American living in Egypt during the time of the outbreak of the 1967 Middle East war. Brother DuBois is well qualified to write such a book, having spent thirteen years in Africa as a journalist and having lived for most of the time in Cairo, Egypt.*

The following chapter describes Suliman's reaction to and his problems revolving around Egypt's pronouncement that all Americans must leave the country due to the outbreak of war between Israel and Egypt.

I must have just fallen asleep. I had listened to more reports on the fighting from Moscow, London, Washington, and Montreal. I'd picked up an English transmission from Bonn and another from Johannesburg. It was about 1:30 a.m. when I finally got into bed. The clock beside my bed now said a little after two. I had no idea how long the telephone had been ringing, but it kept it up persistently as I dragged myself out of the bed and out of the beginnings of deep sleep. My mumbled "hellow" was answered with a shout.

"Where you been!?" Before I could answer, "They're holdin' me! Won't let me out! Say they're gain'na ship me out! Man, you got to get over here, now!" It was Suliman. But I hardly recognized his voice. It was shrill and frightened. He was screaming into the receiver, rushing through his words as if someone were standing beside him threatening to grab the instrument out of his hand. "Man, d'ya hear me!? I been in a fuckin' jail two hours! Nobody'll listen to me!" His voice sounded like he was about to burst out crying. "Man, you got to get over here now, right now! An' get me outta here. The motherfuckers gonna ship me outta Egypt!" He paused.

"Yeah, but where are you?" I asked, shouting too.

"What's the name of this fucking place?" he asked someone. "The Nile Hotel . . . in Garden City," he said almost immediately. "Man, you comin'?"

"Yeah, I'm coming. I'll be there right away. I was asleep when . . ."

" . . . an' bring your shit with you! You'll need it to get into this place. Man, hurry up!" He hung up.

It took me nearly forty-five minutes to get to the Nile Hotel. I walked or rather ran nearly all the way, and was almost breathless when I arrived. I was stopped once on the way. My press card with the attached, recently issued special press privilege stamp had not been questioned. It worked at the door of the hotel, also, where two Black uniformed, armed policemen stood guard. The normally sparkling and revealing tall glass facade of this recently opened hotel was now completely covered with wide strips of heavy blue paper. It looked foreboding.

Despite the hour the plush, high-ceilinged lobby was brightly lit and alive with activity. But, it was apparent immediately that it was not the activity of the tourist hotel lobby it was. There was nothing gay, bright, or leisurely in the atmosphere. People sat or moved about nervously, unsmiling and tense. For the most part they wore dull, mismatched, practical clothes. Many of the women were in slacks. Their usually carefully made-up faces had been carelessly administered to. The always meticulous, if drably attired men were in shirtsleeves and without ties. Disorderly piles of luggage, included hastily fastened cardboard boxes, large paper-wrapped objects of odd shape, and pet carriers of various sizes and shapes. Cigarette butts overflowed the ashtrays and protruded in ugly, bent forms out of the soil of potted plants. Harsh, American-accented English surrounded me.

I approached the reception desk to the right of the entrance, behind which three harassed Egyptians were striving to maintain the cool nonchalance typical of Egypt's first class hotel service personnel—often their cover for inefficiency. They were not succeeding. Affecting my best American stance, I asked:

"Where can I find an American? His name is Suliman Ibn Ismael."

"He's an American?" the young man asked incredulously.

"Yes," I answered without elaborating.

"How long has he been here?" He took up a typed list that lay on the counter in front of him.

"I think he just came in, maybe about an hour or two ago."

"In that case you'd better look in the lobby or upstairs in the lounge or the bar. He may not have been given a room yet. Just a moment." He ran a finger down the list. "Is he suppose to be evacuated?"

"Well, I guess so," I said. "Isn't that what all these people are here for?" Egyptians are masters at asking questions to which the answer is obvious. It's their way of extending conversation and thus the human contact. But, he ignored my question. It had been impolite.

"Oh, yes. Here he is," he said, looking up and smiling. "Suliman Ibn Ismael, employee of the U.S. Food for Development Mission. Yes. He has not been given a room yet, so you'll find him somewhere around the hotel."

"Thank you," I said and turned to leave the counter. As I did so I saw Suliman. He was bobbing down the steps into the lobby beside an official-looking Egyptian who had a sheaf of papers in his hand. A little behind them came an American in shirtsleeves, also carrying a handful of papers. Suliman carried his briefcase, which was open, his passport, a copy of his book, and several newspaper clippings in one hand. The other was occupied with his cane. They turned in the direction of the counter. At that moment Suliman saw me and broke away from them, almost at a run. His face was ashen, its usual sheen gone. His small eyes bulged unnaturally. Their look was piercing. A woman rose from a chair in their path as they crossed the lobby and engaged the two officials in conversation. Before he reached me and ignoring my half-extended hand, Suliman said:

"Man, you know folks around this town! You gotta help me get out of here! Call 'em! Get in touch with 'em! Do anything! But, get me outta this place! What took you so long?" Not waiting for an answer, "Dig, I just talked to the Egyptian cat that's in charge. Says he got my name on a list. He's got some whitey from the embassy with him who's got a list too. Says there's nothing he can do. Said in the morning somebody from Egyptian security will be here I can talk to." He half raised the hand in which he held his briefcase and papers. "Told him about all my shit! Showed him the telegram from Nasser, my clippings, everything! He didn't give a fuck! I even tol' the cat I volunteered for the Egyptian Army; showed him the letter I wrote, everything. Cat said he was sorry, but my name was on the list they got from the fuckin' American embassy!" We were standing at the counter. The clerk with whom I had talked was listening intently, as if it was his right. I took Suliman's arm and led him toward two empty chairs.

"Look Suliman, what exactly happened?" I asked. "You said on the phone you'd been in jail. Have you been home, or what?" We were now seated.

"They stopped me on the way to Mika's. Asked to see my identity card. When I showed 'em my passport they wouldn't give it back and said I'd have to come with them. Took me to the police station on Sarwat Street . . . told me to sit down and disappeared with my passport. They wouldn't tell me nothing. After a while I got mad and started raising hell, until some officer came out. He tol' me not to worry, there was nothing wrong. It was just a check because I was out late, and shit like that. But, the mother didn't give me back my passport, and he disappeared. After a while he came out and said everything was all right, but that I shouldn't be walking in the streets at that hour and they would take me in a police car.

"Man, they put me in this jeep an' before I knew what was happening, they had dumped my ass here!" He had begun the story calmly, but now his voice was beginning to rise. "The cat still hadn't given me my passport. Gave it to that dude over there," indicating the Egyptian he'd entered the lobby with and who was now talking with the clerks at the counter. "They planning to ship my ass outta here, man! I tol' the cat everything. He says he can't do nothing 'til this important cat from security comes in the morning. Says not to worry or get mad. But, man, you gotta do something! They can't keep me here with all these whities!"

I looked up at the approach of the Egyptian official. "You'll be in room 813, Mr. Suliman," he said pleasantly. "The clerk at the counter will give you the key." He eyed me suspiciously as he continued. "Don't worry about anything. Everything's going to be all right."

"This is Mr. Bob Jones," Suliman said, rising. "He's a friend. He's going to see if he can help too." To me he said: "This is Mr. Munir." I stood up and took his hand. There was a question in his expression and manner, but he said only, "Hellow." And then to Suliman: "I'll see you in the morning," and left us. As I sat down I watched him join his American colleague who was still talking with the woman that had stopped them. They spoke to each other, both glancing in my direction, and then compared lists intently. I was sure they were looking for my name.

"I saw Kamal's name on the list," Suliman said. "It was above mine. And Hank's is there too, and Ibrahim's. Cat said they'll probably be comin' here sometime tomorrow. D'ya know that Mohammed left a week ago? Cut out to Addis Ababa, jus' like that. Didn't nobody know he was goin'. He must of knew the shit was going to break."

"Karima came to see me tonight," I said as matter-of-factly as I could. "Looking for you. Says she heard they were shipping out Americans. Came with Sayyid. Thought they'd find you at my place."

"Man, damn that chick. I been givin' her money. Ain't nothing I can do until I get outta here!" He sat forward in his chair. "Listen. First thing in the morning you got to go see Mr. Mursy at the Islamic Center. Man, you got to be there early . . . when he comes in. Tell him they holding me here and plannin' to ship me out . . ."

"But, nobody's likely to be in their offices tomorrow," I said weakly. "And, even if they are, they won't be in early." The look of betrayal in his eyes compelled me to add, "Malesh . . . I'll go early, first thing and see."

"You got contacts in the office of the minister of culture," he continued. "They printed one of my poems in their magazine. See them. They won't let me do it here, but when you leave now, tonight, you gotta send a telegram to Nasser, tellin' him they holding me." In response to the surprised look on my face, he urged: "Man, you got to do it! There ain't much time!"

"But," I hesitated, "There's a war on . . . an' the Egyptians've been hit bad. Nobody knows where Nasser is! I'll send the telegram, if I can. But, don't count on it working."

"Jus' send it, and tell Mr. Mursy you sent it," he said. "He'll get the hint. He can stop 'em from kicking me out. I know it, an' he'll do it. You jus' gotta get to him first thing in the morning. I got his telephone number at the apartment. If I had it here I'd call him, myself, right now."

"What are you suppose to do about your things and the apartment?"

"They said tomorrow they'd send somebody with me, like a guard, to the apartment while I packed clothes and things and brought them back over here. I'm jus' suppose to leave the apartment. Ain't that some shit?! I called Mika and told her. She was still waiting for me. She said she'd be here in the morning. She was packing when I talked to her. I couldn't talk long. Wasn't suppose to make no calls, the cat told me. But, I raised so much hell he let me."

Our attention was caught by a commotion at the entrance to the hotel. A smartly dressed police officer had let in a group of young people that we immediately recognized as students from the American University. Hank was in their midst, dressed in a mode-cut dark suit, in sharp contrast to the others, and affecting that lost and helpless attitude he'd had when I first saw him in midtown Cairo. Blue-gowned porters loaded down with luggage followed. Suliman jumped up and went off in the direction of the group. I rose and followed.

"Hey, brother," Suliman called out as we approached Hank. "They got you too?" The question was serious.

"Yeah," Hank smiled. "I wouldn't miss no free trip to Greece. Ain't this some shit!" We shook hands, Hank keeping languid but at the same time watchful eyes on the porters and his luggage.

"Well, you can bet your sweet ass I ain't goin'," Suliman said without smiling.

"Inshallah," I interjected, placing his destiny in the hands of God.

As if caught off guard by an inferior opponent, Suliman repeated aggressively but unconvincingly: "Inshallah."

I Am We

by Huey P. Newton

n this brief, brilliant statement taken from Revolutionary Suicide, *Huey P. Newton further clarifies the concept of revolutionary suicide—the common struggle and oneness of all humankind.*

There is an old African saying, "I am we." If you met an African in ancient times and asked him who he was, he would reply, "I am we." This is revolutionary suicide: I, we, all of us are the one and the multitude.

So many of my comrades are gone now. Some tight partners, crime partners, and brothers off the block are begging on the street. Others are in asylum, penitentiary, or grave. They are all suicides of one kind or another who had the sensitivity and tragic imagination to see the oppression. Some overcame; they are the revolutionary suicides. Others were reactionary suicides who either overestimated or underestimated the enemy, but in any case were powerless to change their conception of the oppressor.

The difference lies in hope and desire. By hoping and desiring, the revolutionary suicide chooses life; he is, in the words of Nietzsche, "an arrow of longing for another shore." Both suicides despise tyranny, but the revolutionary is both a great despiser and a great adorer who longs for another shore. The reactionary suicide must learn, as his brother the revolutionary has learned, that the desert is not a circle. It is a spiral. When we have passed through the desert, nothing will be the same.

You cannot bare your throat to the murderer. As George Jackson said, you must defend yourself and take the dragon position as in karate and make the

Huey P. Newton receives his PhD from the University of California, Santa Cruz, 1980. Photographer unknown.

front kick and the back kick when you are surrounded. You do not beg because your enemy comes with the butcher knife in one hand and the hatchet in the other. "He will not become a Buddhist overnight."

The Preacher said that the wise man and the fool have the same end; they go to the grave as a dog. Who sends us to the grave? The unknowable, the force that dictates to all classes, all territories, all ideologies; he is death, the Big Boss. An ambitious man seeks to dethrone the Big Boss, to free himself, to control when and how he will go to the grave.

There is another illuminating story of the wise man and the fool found in *Mao's Little Red Book*: A foolish old man went to North Mountain and began to dig; a wise old man passed by and said, "Why do you dig, foolish old man? Do you not know that you cannot move the mountain with a little shovel?" But the foolish old man answered resolutely, "While the mountain cannot get any higher, it will get lower with each shovelful. When I pass on, my sons and his sons and his son's sons will go on making the mountain lower. Why can't we move the mountain?" And the foolish old man kept digging, and the generations that followed after him, and the wise old man looked on in disgust. But the resoluteness and the spirit of the generations that followed the foolish old man touched God's heart, and God sent two angels who put the mountain on their backs and moved the mountain.

This is the story Mao told. When he spoke of God he meant the six hundred million who had helped him to move imperialism and bourgeois thinking, the two great mountains.

The reactionary suicide is "wise," and the revolutionary suicide is a "fool," a fool for the revolution in the way that Paul meant when be spoke of being "a fool for Christ." That foolishness can move the mountain of oppression; it is our great leap and our commitment to the dead and the unborn.

We will touch God's heart; we will touch the people's heart, and together we will move the mountain.

I Know Who You Are

I know who you are
I've seen what you do
Your smile has a way
Of soothing a wound
The face of the man
Who'd make all men free
Is the face of the man
Who says he loves me

You're the free man
That is, the man
Who can make us free
You're THE man
And, you're my man
Forever . . .

I know who you are
I know of your pain
You've seen all your people
In shackles and chains
But you know what to do
Yes, I swear that you do
Yes, I swear that you do
You will make them be free
Just as you've made me

You're the free man
That is, the man
Who can make us free
You're THE man
And, you're my man
Forever . . .

I know who you are
I know where you've been
So you'll go where you must
Fight to the end
But do what you do
I know you have to
And I'll be along
'Cause you've made me strong

You're the free man
That is, the man
Who can make us free
You're THE man
And, you're my man
Forever . . .

Afterword

How Did You Guys Start
All Those Programs?

The original vision of the Black Panther Party was structured by the practical needs of the people, not by rhetoric and ideology. The failure of city and federal administrators to address the basic needs of the community was the reason we created our survival programs. This book serves as a model for social change movements and so-called "progressive" political leaders to shift the focus from feel-good speeches, entertainment, and publicity to concrete action and the implementation of sorely needed service programs for the people.

We formed the Black Panther Party because we wanted to liberate our community. While we were very young and inexperienced, we overcame many obstacles on the path to building our organization. Party members implemented the survival programs, and our "Service to the People" model became a tool by which we educated the masses. Huey Newton, leader of our party, said that the survival programs were "not revolutionary nor reformist but a tactic and strategy by which we organized the people." We understood that in order to transform society it was first necessary to survive economic and social oppression.

Our experiences in the Black Panther Party offer many important lessons for our communities. Many of the issues facing the economically disadvantaged today are the same as they were in the '60s and '70s. Billions of dollars are spent on the war in Iraq while our schools are underfunded, millions of American citizens are denied basic health care, many lack jobs paying decent wages, and crime is rampant in our communities. This book makes the case for the Black Panther Survival Programs as a model to address some of these basic social injustices and economic problems. It is a practical guide for all the students and activists who continually ask, "How did you guys start all those programs?"

David Hilliard